PLAYING HARDBALL

"Oil, oil, oil! Doesn't anyone ever talk about baseball anymore?"

Lawrence Frank

PLAYING HARDBALL

The Dynamics of Baseball Folk Speech

Peter Lang

New York • Berne • Frankfort on the Main

Library of Congress Cataloging in Publication Data

Frank, Lawrence, 1960–
    Playing hardball.

    Bibliography: p.
    1. Baseball – United States – Folklore.   2. Baseball –
United States – Terminology.   3. English language – Terms
and phrases.   4. Baseball players – United States – Folk-
lore.   I. Title.
GR105.F73   1984   398'.355   83-48834
ISBN 0-8204-0061-0

Cover Photograph:
Professor Harold Edgerton
Massachusetts Institute of Technology

Cover Design:
C.M. Kuss/Connections Information Service, Inc.

Illustrations:
Carrie Wieseneck

Typesetting & Design:
Connections Information Service, Inc.
Cambridge, MA

Printed by Lang Druck Ltd., Liebefeld/Berne (Switzerland)

To my parents

Contents

Foreword

This book on baseball folk speech underscores and sustains the essential character of the game and its distinctive Americanism.

Baseball has stood the test of changing history, of political change and technological advances. It is forever resilient, having adjusted to night games and to artificial turf, and having survived Charlie Finley.

The reason is not a matter of accident. It is a matter of the essence of the game: baseball is different from other games. Its strength is inherent, metaphysical. Why? First, because the game has a singular and distinctive relationship to time. Only baseball, among all games, can be called a "pastime." For baseball is above or outside time. Football, basketball, hockey, soccer games are arbitrarily divided into measured quarters, halves, or periods. They are controlled, even dominated by time. Not so baseball, which either ignores time or dominates it. An inning theoretically can go on forever. The same is true of the game. Interruptions are generally limited to acts of God, such as darkness or rain, or to cultural, religious and quasi-natural occurrences such as curfew or midnight (in the case of night games). In baseball, if a game must be halted "time out" is not taken, with referees looking at their watches. Rather time is "called" by the umpire. Again theoretically, time once called could be "called" forever.

Baseball is also played in a unique spatial frame. Other games are restricted to limited, defined areas, rectangular or near rectangular, floors or rinks. Not so baseball. Baseball is played within the lines of a projection from home plate, starting from the point of a 90° and extending to infinity. Were it not for the intervention of fences, buildings, mountains, and other obstacles in space, a baseball traveling within the ultimate projection of the first and third baselines could be fair and fully and infinitely in play. Baseballs never absolutely go out of bounds. They are either fair or foul; and even foul balls are, within limits, playable and part of the game.

Baseball is distinguished from other games, too in the way in which it is controlled by umpires. An umpire is very different from a referee, a field judge, or a linesman. One occasionally hears the cry "fire the referee" but seldom the cry "kill the referee." That cry is reserved for umpires. Umpires have to be dealt with absolutely, for their power is absolute. Referees are men called or appointed. Umpires, by contrast, seem to exist in their own right and exercise undelegated power which is not to be reviewed and from which there is no appeal. Umpires are not asked to make judgments. They make them. The name itself carries great strength. It is derived from the Old French *"noumpere,"* meaning one who is alone or without peer (literally without father). "Refuse not," the medieval divines warned, "the umpeership and judgments of the Holy Ghoste."

Baseball is different from other major sports in two other significant ways. First, the individual player is under constant surveillance and clearly responsible. And, second, baseball is a game of records, team and individual. The bookkeeping of baseball is balanced. It shows earned runs and unearned runs; hits are credited to batters and debited to pitchers. Errors are recorded along with assists and put-outs. The game is played for the game, for the day, but also for the record, and for eternity.

And its language, too, as Lawrence Frank in this book writes and demonstrates, is beyond temporal and passing significance. It reflects, or better shows, the nature of the game: its metaphysical purity, its detachment from the passing and temporal, its continuing and abiding strength — as Latin was used to hold theology in certainty and French the law.

EUGENE J. MCCARTHY

Preface

The data in this study were collected between 1979 and 1983 while the author was playing for the Novato Knicks, a semi-pro team located in Novato, California. The team was a member of the Sacramento Rural League which consisted of teams from Northern California. Like most of the other teams in the league, the Novato Knicks consisted primarily of the most skilled of the former local high school players who wanted to continue playing baseball competitively, and local college players keeping in shape during the summer months. Most teams had a few players that had previously played at some level of professional ball. The ages of the players ranged, approximately, from 18 years to 27 years. The games were played on weekends, from May through August, to accommodate players who worked or were in college. For the players, baseball provided a source of play. The players were not paid. Most of the spectators were relatives and girlfriends of the players and a few locals that followed the the progress of the city team.

Acknowledgments

I would like to thank the entire Novato Knicks team who helped me, for the most part unknowingly, in the collection of my data. Also very helpful in providing data were Mike Lopez, Russ Hatt, and Steve Bovaird of the Knicks, Victor Guinasso, former pitcher for the University of San Francisco, and Ken Siler, former pitcher for the Salem (Oregon) Senators of the Single A Northwest League as well as a former Knick teammate. I would like to thank Dr. Robert Lichtenstein for reading the original mauscript. I would also like to thank Prof. Gardener Stout for graciously providing me with the time to complete my study, my parents for their support in many more ways than just financial, Sandy Rauch for organizing my burdensome academic affairs, and Carrie for organizing the rest. The cover photograph was generously donated by Prof. Harold "Doc" Edgerton, to whom I am grateful. Above all, I thank my mentor, Prof. Alan Dundes, who first suggested that I work on the project and whose inspiration, guidance, and confidence in my work made this book possible.

"... a certain ancient game, played with a ball, hath come up again, yet already are all mouths filled with the phrases that describe its parts and movement; insomuch, indeed, that the ears of the sober and such as would busy themselves with weightier matter are racked with the clack of the same till they do ache with anguish."

Mark Twain
"An Extract from Methuselah's Diary"

INTRODUCTION

In the August 21st issue of *The Nation* in 1913, an article appeared that discussed the growing concern that the use of the language of baseball in the newspapers was resulting in a decrease in "graphic description" in favor of "hysterical slang". It pointed to the fact that the "sporting pages" of certain newspapers (*Nation* 1913) "actually have to be of a different color from the rest of the edition in order to stand the strain of the verbal whirlwind which daily strews them with linguistic wreckage."

This movement to reform the language that was being used by the baseball journalists of the time seems to have been headed, according to *The Washington Post,* by a certain Professor McClintock of the University of Chicago, who was presumably asking the same question that *The Nation* had asked: "Why is it that when it essays to tell what happened at the Polo Grounds or Ebbets Field between the hours of 3:30 and 6 P.M., the English language stands on its head and tries to convey its meaning by waving its hands and feet, instead of speaking like one sane man to another?" Apparently, this fear of the "Peril of the Baseball Lingo" (*Literary Digest* 1913) did not last long. By 1927 there had grown a fascination with the language of baseball and the "hysterical slang" was beginning to be described as "noble descriptive terms", in the words of Gretchen Lee, writing in *American Speech* in 1926 (Lee 1926).

Today, the language of baseball has infiltrated the speech of so many Americans that little notice is taken when someone voices their agreement by saying "You're batting a thousand!" or when a person whose judgement is in error is said to be "way off base". In fact, because of the fairly recent popularity of the game of "softball" (a toned-down derivative of baseball that is played with a larger, softer ball and is often not so competitive in spirit), the distinction between something that is done for fun and something that is done very seriously is often compared to the difference between these two sports. Someone who is performing a task with vigor, completeness, and intentions of victory is said to be "playing hardball". Among the baseball players themselves, there are hundreds of terms that are used both on and off of the playing field. The focus of this book, however, is not on baseball terms. While there is indeed a good deal of baseball slang that has become known to the general public and is standard equipment to the sports journalist and television commentator, it is often forgotten that it is the baseball players themselves that are at the core of the development of such slang. It is important to study the speech of the players, not the journalists. The speech of players that is used during games includes a great deal more than just descriptive terms. The verbal expressions used by baseball players arise not only from the need to describe objects or situations particular to the game, but also from the interactions of the players.

In order to fully understand the array of folk expressions of a group, it is essential to study the nature of that group in detail. While this may seem fairly obvious, it is surprising how many studies of baseball slang have been done without a thorough understanding of the players and the game. The task of studying groups of people is a primary concern of the field of folklore. For the reader of this book, it will be important to understand the usefulness of modern folklore studies in analyzing cultural phenomena. Therefore, there is attention paid to explaining some of the general concepts of folklore. Of course, it is not possible to do justice to the entire discipline of folklore in only a few pages. Readers interested in learning more about the subject of folklore are urged to read, among other works, Jan Harold Brunvand's *The Study of American Folklore* (Brunvand 1978) or Alan Dundes' *The Study of Folklore* (Dundes 1965). These works give a thorough treatment of the basics of the subject and provide helpful bibliographies.

The purpose of this book, then, is to try to outline some of the major factors in the development and usage of the folk speech that exists in baseball and arises from the face-to-face interaction of the players. The attempt is made to try to understand both the meaning and the function of particular elements of the folk speech. A large part of the folk speech of players is derogatory in nature. This taunting between opponents and teammates alike, as well as the supportive comments offered to teammates, is a subject that has rarely been studied. The complex system of personal interaction that exists within the structure of a game as complicated as baseball presents the formidable task of interpreting the players responses not only to teammates and opponents, but to the structure of the game itself. This is essential when considering the reason for the existence of particular expressions or "items" of the players' folk speech. Furthermore, it becomes fairly obvious that it is impossible to study baseball folk speech without in some way returning to a study of at least some aspect of American culture. The folk speech of the players can reveal a great deal about the relationship between American culture and the culture of baseball players.

Of course, it is impossible to capture every element of the constantly changing folk speech of any folk group. The attempt has been made to elucidate some of the important features in the development and usage of the folk speech that arise in the complex structure of interaction inherent to the game of baseball. Undoubtedly, though, there is bound to be something that has been missed. These same sentiments were expressed in 1927 by one V. Samuels of Lincoln, Nebraska who, writing in the contributor's column of *American Speech* (Samuels 1927), ended his brief essay entitled "Baseball Slang" with words that are as appropriate now as they were then; "Very likely other words, phrases, or locations should be added which I do not recall as I write."

Chapter 1
DYNAMIC AMERICANA

"Whoever wants to know the heart and mind of America had better learn baseball."

Jacques Barzun

One of the least studied of American folk groups is baseball players. The sport hailed as our "national game" has received little serious attention from folklorists, possibly because of the recurring problem that folklorists have in acknowledging folk groups indigenous to their own cultures. If baseball is as true a representation as Jacques Barzun suggested (Barzun 1964:5), then surely the study of the game and its players can be a revealing look at many features of American culture. The majority of attempts that have been made to understand the game of baseball have been from the viewpoint of the spectator. It is from the perspective of the players, though, that one is best able to study the nature of the game and its participants. In general, this approach is essential to the study of any folk group. One cannot hope to understand aspects of a culture unless an attempt is made to understand that culture from the viewpoint of someone from that particular culture. The

5

study of baseball folk speech can provide a useful method of revealing patterns of personal interaction that reflect both the conscious and unconscious dimensions of conflict and support that arise in the game of baseball and in American culture itself.

Because people often consider the term "folk" to pertain to other cultures, they tend to overlook the folkloric elements of our own society. Most people seem to retain the nineteenth century definition of "folklore" as something related to an old-fashioned, backward, and remote group of rural people whose lifestyle is so different that, for all intents and purposes, they are foreigners to most Americans. With them is often associated the notion of illiteracy. This is far too narrow a view, however. Modern folklore studies have made great progress in broadening people's concept of exactly what "folklore" is, and who the "folk" are. Folklore need not be associated only with the songs of an old family in the Ozarks, but also with the events and interactions of our everyday life.[1]

In attempting to study the folklore of a particular group of people, one must first decide what makes them a "folk group". Much of the progress in modern folklore studies has arisen as a result of the redefinition of the folk group in an attempt not only to encompass a far more diverse collection of peoples, but to recognize distinct groups of people that exist within larger societies. This is particularly important in the case of American culture where ethnic, occupational, and even recreational diversity, among other things, results in a great variety of groups of people with cultural characteristics peculiar to the particular group to which they belong. First of all, it is necessary to have a useful definition of exactly what a folk group is. A folk group can be defined as "any group of people whatsoever who share at least one common factor" (Dundes 1965:2) The "linking factor" may be language, occupation, religion, ethnicity, or, in our case, the participation in the sport of baseball. With this definition, it is apparent that the world around us abounds in folk groups; many which need certainly not be rural, backward, nor old-fashioned. This modern definition of the folk group has greatly enhanced the usefulness of folklore as a study of our own culture. The folk are no longer just "them" but also "us".

The members of a folk group often develop specialized aspects of their language or linguistic habits that pertain to the function that defines them as a folk group. The study of a group's "folk speech" can reveal a great deal about that particular group. It is in studying the folk speech of a group that one can best deduce patterns in human interaction and thus come a step closer to understanding the people who comprise that group. People are continually being exposed to the folk speech of various groups, though they may not realize it. Who has not heard, at one time or another, a politician say that two groups are not fighting but, instead, are "in a conflict situation"? One of the most fascinating examples of the development and usage of a "folk speech" of a group is that exhibited by baseball players. What makes the folk speech of baseball players so fascinating is not just its originality, wit, and vitality but the fact that it is a reflection of a sport that is very much a part of the lives of many Americans. Baseball is ingrained in American culture and the study of its folklore can be an interesting look into American culture itself. Through the study of the folk speech of baseball players, it is possible to get an interesting perspective on American values, behavior, and psychology.

Before studying the specifics of the folk group of baseball players, then, it is important to understand the connection between the game and the American society in which it is embedded. Why is it that Americans find baseball so intriguing? Though it is a fascinating sport, the interest our nation has in it seems to go beyond mere spectator curiosity. I propose that the continuing interest in the sport of baseball is due, in part, to the similarities that people see in baseball and American society — similarities not only in values and attitudes, but in the structure of human interaction. Furthermore, it is possible that the resemblance in the historical development of baseball and its rise to social respectability, and the strivings of America in the mid-1800's and early 1900's to become a powerful and respected nation, are attractive aspects of the game, appealing to our patriotism.

The development of folk speech traditions in baseball are rooted in the early days of the game when America itself was striving to become respectable. In his article "The Question of Folklore in a New Nation," (reprinted in Dorson 1971:94-107) Richard Dorson discusses the conscious effort of early Americans to distinguish American speech from the English speech that settlers had brought over from England in the seventeenth century. He points out that "novel styles of expression were forming among the novel breeds of settlers, and from the 1820's on their 'tall' and 'cute' talk, comic imagery, bold metaphors, and homespun rhythms" were a much noted phenomemon. Many of these traits were to carry over into the speech of the players of the game of baseball, which was to appear around 1850. Indeed, as Lawrence Ritter points out in his wonderful book *The Glory of Their Times* (Ritter 1966:xvi), the early baseball players were much like the early settlers of America; "They were pioneers, in every sense of the word, engaged in a pursuit in which only the most skilled, the most determined, and, above all, the most rugged survived. They entered an endeavor which lacked social respectability, and when they left it, it was America's National Game." So, from its inception, the baseball community has to some degree mirrored the American society. Baseball, in its early days, presented a dynamic representation of the American spirit.

It expressed "the exuberance and unbounded optimism of a nation confident of its ability to shape the future to its will and mold its own destiny." (Ritter 1966:xvi) It is not surprising, then, that the historical aspect is an important element of the whole ethos of the game. It is important, then, to consider this influence.

In the early days of the game, baseball players were primarily members of the lower class. Baseball players were considered, according to New York Giants catcher Chief Meyers, "a rowdy bunch" and, in the words of one Reverend Jonathan Townley Crane, "everyone connected with it (baseball) seems to be regarded with a degree of suspicion." (quoted in Smith 1975:2). Apparently, as Douglass Wallop points out in his book *Baseball: An Informal History* (Wallop 1969), these statements were not far from the truth. Baseball did manage to clean itself up and as the game came into national prominence it began to provide a link between the lower class and the emerging upper class. Players, who most often were from rather poor backgrounds, began making large amounts of money and the affluent as well as the poor were being attracted to the ballpark to watch the games. More importantly, though, baseball provided American heroes. And this influence of admiration played an important role in the cultural development of the nation. Dorson describes the importance of the hero in American culture, stating that "As the nation needed a mythological founder-hero and father-figure like (George) Washington, so it craved more intimate, popular demigods to identify with its down-to-earth American traits and sky-soaring American ambitions." (Dorson 1971:100). Baseball provided us with Babe Ruth. The mythologizing of Babe Ruth represented the search for a national identity and helped ingrain baseball in the nation's heritage. Through Ruth, baseball became an expression of the abundance of America's opportunities. It was a game, yet its players, mostly lower class people, had the chance to emerge as national figures and achieve financial success. In this sense, the baseball heroes transcended the sporting world.

It is in this sense that Babe Ruth is a true American folk hero. He represented the American ideal of "big"; he himself was large, he brought the big hit (the home run) into popularity, and he made lots of money. He exhibited truly "American" character traits; he drank and he womanized, yet he loved children and hot dogs. He was truly a Yankee. In a time of depression he represented a figure who could exist both in the elite world of the wealthy and in the common man's world of bawdiness and play. His reign in the national game made him the figurehead of the pastime that, according to Mark Twain, had been "the very symbol, the outward struggle of the raging, tearing, booming nineteenth century" (Twain 1948:323) and, as James Reston wrote, "a unifying social force, and a counter to the confusion about the vagueness and complexity of our cities" (Reston 1966) in the twentieth century. Thus "The Babe" himself became more than just a baseball star, but a man who had risen out of the amorphous conglomeration of common people to achieve fame and money, and a place amongst the upper classes, while still retaining the vitality, the enthusiasm, and the playfulness of his early years. In this he represented not only the American dream of wealth, but, more generally, the concept of America as a homeland. The Babe grew up poor and in a boys home only to become the father figure to many American youths.

The idolization of Babe Ruth may also have its roots in the structure of games in general. Through participation in a game, Ruth was able to become as prominent a figure as the politicians of the time. This national stature can be seen as a result of the place and function of games in our society. As psychoanalyst Erik Erikson points out in his book *Toys and Reason, Stages in the Ritualization of Experience,* "games stand midway between individual play in the toy world and the arena of politics in which human beings unite in communal interplay and establish rules for joining and for contesting with each other. Each such polis, too, is governed by a shared vision according to which a pre-ordained type of man enjoys a maximum of individual leeway (now called freedom) within a legalized system of traditional antagonisms." (Erikson 1977:72) The idoliz-ation of Ruth, then, may be seen as a way in which he transcended the game stage and ascended to the political arena. This had the effect of elevating the interests of the common man to national importance and demystifying the image of the untouchable politician. And it was Ruth himself that was able to express this with humble jocularity in explaining that the reason why he had earned more money than President Hoover was that "I had a better year."

Yet, even though the rich heritage of the sport is undoubtedly one of the charms of the game, the continuing attraction that Americans feel toward baseball is not due to purely nostaglic considerations. More importantly, the structure of the game itself and the values of the community of baseball players hold a close resemblence to American society, yet within the context of a sport and thus closer to the attractive world of play. It is a game composed of individuals whose success as a group depends on both their individual abilities and their cooperation within the framework of a team. The result, as Michael Novak astutely points out in *The Joy of Sports,* is that individual honor and dignity are stressed within a context of associational cooperation. The game further reflects American culture in that it is, in the words of Novak, "orderly, reasoned, judiciously balanced, incorporating segments of violence and collision in a larger plan of rationality, absolutely dependent on an interiorization of public rules." (Novak 1976:58) Yet within these rules are an infinitude of physical and statistical variations. And, as Allen Guttman deduces, because of the spatial separation of the players, it is

possible to quantify almost every aspect of the game
(Guttman 1978:109). As both Novak and Guttman point
out, baseball shares the American interest in quantification, which, to some degree, is concomitant with the
American capitalist system (Brohm 1972:23). Such concepts are reflected in the folk speech of the players. A player
who has a batting average of .150 is often said to be "hitting
a buck-fifty"; accomplishments in the field have been
transformed into equivalent financial rewards. Furthermore, the definite pastoral impulse is baseball (Guttman
1978:100) is attractive to the American society that in
becoming increasingly more urbanized.

Baseball is the perfect confluence of athletics and
intelligence that seems to intrigue Americans. The plethora
of rules, statistics, and strategic information that are part
of the game lend baseball an air of almost mystical
complexity, in which the role of chance and luck emerge as
formidable opponents to the seemingly rigid structure of
the game. The following quotation from a 1908 edition of
Baseball Magazine shows that even in the early years of the
game this similarity in American society and the game of
baseball resulted in a special interest in the game:
"Baseball is not merely an interesting and scientific game.
It is the game which calls into play the dominant traits of
Americans in its demand for agility, quick thinking, and a
tremendous exertion and excitement." (Wallop 1969:50-51)
The interest Americans have in baseball may reflect their
interest in study and statistics, as well as in the observance
of social movement controlled by a pretext of winning and
losing, made even more attractive because the distance of
the spectator lends an air of voyeurism. Also, many
Americans have played baseball in their youth. And even if
one did not play baseball, it is likely that a game was played
in which certain aspects and specific skills of baseball
existed. So even if you never played the game of baseball,
you played part of it — "fly out", "pickle", "pepper", etc. If

there is anything that draws one's interest to a game, it is having participated in it, or at least something like it.

From this overall structure of a game that encompasses a high degree of both physical and mental activity arises other connections with American culture. Though some are less obvious, they still are a further representation of the overall mode of thinking that is common to both. For instance, in American society there exists a certain pride in being able to buck the system and obtain an advantage by getting around rules and regulations by both mental and physical agility. The popularity of fictional characters such as James Bond, 007, are due, in part, to the fascination people have with these characters' abilities to conquer their opponent with often elaborate deception getting by security systems, using tricky devices, etc. The intrigue of deception exists in baseball too. Though the game is played under a strict set of rules, there is a joy in being able to defeat the system by various means of stretching the rules. For instance, a batter may try to move his back foot slightly out of the back of the batter's box so as to have that extra split second to judge the position of the pitches. Sometimes overtly illegal means are used, such as a pitcher cutting the ball to make his pitches dip wildly or, for the same purpose using foreign substances on the ball — a "spitball" perhaps. There is even a sense in which trickery well done is applauded as a masterful act, as in a "phantom double play", where the foot of the defensive man attempting to complete a double play does not actually touch second base but skims over it in an attempt to avoid the oncoming runner and still get off a strong throw to first base. In this case the quickness and elegance of the shortstop (or second baseman) is considered an athletic act of deception at the expense of the umpire. Even the baseball field itself may be slightly altered to the home team's advantage. If a team has many good bunters, they may have the groundskeepers slant the dirt near the foul lines towards the infield so that bunts have a better chance staying in fair territory.[2]

Novak's "associational" game and Guttman's "quantized pastoral" both describe elements that are indeed important to the overall ethos of the game. Yet the one aspect of the game that both authors overlook is precisely that which most folklorists have neglected: the dimension of conflict between the opposing teams within this "cerebral" game. This is a crucial consideration if the game is to be studied from the player's point of view, as it should be. Because of the inherent agonistic relationship between teams, the pastoral element of the game contains a strong undercurrent of feudal conflict in which two teams engage in a symbolic struggle to retain possession of the field their homeland. The game becomes a contest to protect the "field", the home, against an opposing group of male attackers. It is important to try to interpret how the structure of the game affects the folk speech of the players. Although the game is always approached with the premise that the bases belong to the offensive team, the folk speech of the players reveals that it is more appropriate to consider the bases as belonging to the defensive team. (Why else would the offensive team have to "steal" them?) Thus the fact that players are "safe" when occupying a base is not only an expression of their invulnerability when on the base but also a way of marking the progress that the offensive team has made into the enemy zone; a further quantification in a game in which events — good or bad — become facts. Almost every aspect of the game is, in some manner, kept track of statistically. This notion of progress into enemy territory is also apparent in the symbolic use by American youths of the four bases as representative of different stages of sexual activity (Wentworth 1967). This particular usage underscores the association that is apparent in many folk expressions between sexual dominance and the literal physical advancement into the opponent's territory.

Though the question of who "owns" the bases may appear to be a trivial philosophical point of contention, it is crucial in understanding the folk speech that arises during games. The folk speech of players during game situations contains many images of home life that reflect this symbolic feudal conflict. Furthermore, structurally speaking, this form of traditional vocal expression closely resembles verbal dueling in that physical dominance in the dramatic action of the game is represented as sexual dominance in symbolic verbal form. From this, and the tensions between players' personalities resulting from the fact that they are young males engaged in physical competition, there arises a good deal of homosexual symbolism. This is not to imply, of course, that baseball players are homosexual. That is neither a prerequisite for, nor a conclusion stemming from, such imagery. Instead, it arises from the complex tensions, often unconscious, existing between young males in American culture. It must be kept in mind that in baseball taunting, as in other forms of verbal dueling, "the determining factors involved may not be in the conscious mind of the duel participants" (Dundes 1978:72). This is an important rationale for the psychoanalytic content of this study.[3]

On a larger scale, it is possible that, in a certain sense, baseball exists as an analogue of the ethnic folk groups that exist in America. It is a group of people changing continually with time yet striving to retain the basic elements of social value and structure that delineate the heritage of their progenitors. Baseball enthusiasts are very concerned with remembering the past as well as continually comparing the present with the past. Maybe it is the innate similarity in the emergence of baseball into social respectability, and the strivings of each diverse culture that exists in America to gain recognition and respectability in a society that is continually trying to classify its peoples as simply "Americans", that is responsible for the interest in the culture of baseball. Above all, though, baseball mirrors American culture itself, but within the boundaries, limitations, and rules that exist in the structure of a game, where

conflict exists within a harmless and impersonal environment. Baseball presents a picture of order in the chaotic
modern world. In a world in which "nothing is perfect",
baseball offers us such concepts as the perfect game".[4]

Chapter 2

THE STRUCTURE OF THE GAME

The structure of the game of baseball is a strong influence in the development and usage of the array of folk expressions of its players. The formal structural units of folk speech provide a channel for the expression of verbal control while the structure of the game provides the forum for the assertion of physical control. Since the players perform as individuals, the degree to which they collaborate effectively with teammates depends a great deal on both their vocal and physical cooperation. For instance, every defensive players controls his own portion of the field and must not only interact physically, but communicate effectively, with his teammates if the team as a whole is to be capable defensively. Each player is an important vocal component of his team and thus must develop confidence in his verbal skills. This confidence in vocal expression is manifest in the willingness that players have to "give heat" — taunt — both opponents and teammates.

An inherent quality of baseball that greatly effects the folk speech of its players is the temporal variations of the game. There is a good deal of time when there is no action.

These breaks are often good times for the players to analyze the particular situations and decide on strategies. It is also a prime time for players to yell at the opposition. Furthermore, the players are active in different degrees at different times during the course of a game. In their important work on the structural aspects of games "The Dimensions of Games" (Avedon 1971:408-418), Fritz Redl, Paul Gump, and Brain Sutton-Smith outline "four levels of participation" in games which can be usefully applied to baseball. These levels are "active participation" (e.g., throwing the ball), "in-game passive participation" — watching play until it comes into one's own area of participation (such as the fielders before the ball comes into their area of play), "in-game waiting"; waiting one's turn (such as the hitters before their turns at bat), and "out-of-game waiting" (players not in the line-up).[1] I propose that each of these levels of participation can affect the use of ritualized verbal expression, such as taunting, during the course of a game. Players involved in either of the two classifications of "waiting" require less concentration than those players in "participation" stages and have more time to taunt the opposition. This is an important psychological aspect of the game, as it gives a feeling of involvement to players that are not strictly participating in the actions of the game. In a sense, the players in the "waiting" stages can be effectively elevated to what might be called a "pseudo-participation" stage through the use of ritualized verbal expression. For the player in "in-game waiting", taunting can enhance his attentiveness to the actions of the game in which he must soon partake, and for the player in "out-of-game waiting" it gives a feeling of involvement and purpose.

Since baseball contains all four of these levels, there is a wide variation within the game itself in the usage of folk speech. These levels can influence the proximity of players to one another, the level of concentration on the game, and the amount of competitive conflict with the opposition. All of these are important factors in both the development and usage of the players' folk speech.

The proximity of the players to one another, which is affected by these levels of participation, is an important influence in the use of taunting. For players sitting in the dugout (as opposed to being spread out on the field) there is a greater tendency to taunt the opposition. This effect may be called "spatial enhancement" of slang. By being both an observer and a possible participant, players in the dugout become an "active audience" in the sense that they are involved in the vocal aspect of the game, though not in the physical. For instance, when the offensive team retires to the dugout during their turn on offense, the players are all close together and it is from these players that the most taunting emanates. One of the most important concepts in Redl, Gump, and Sutton-Smith's theory is that the total structure of the game creates an interdependence of the players (Avedon 1971:412). The passage of the ball between fielders, communication between the pitcher and the catcher, and the communication of the runners on the bases, are only some aspects of the game that require that the players have a necessary dependency upon each other. It is possible that the high degree of interdependence in baseball serves to create closer emotional ties among the players, thus raising the communication to a more personal level in which insulting becomes a more affective force.

Taunting that arises during competition against other teams is consonant with the concept of what Redl, Gump, and Sutton-Smith term the structure of "challenge", represented by "actors" and "counter-actors". One of these challenges is "the harassment", in which the actor's purpose is "to tease, taunt, lure to mistake or to unsuccesful attack" whereas the purpose of the counter-actor is "to see through the trick, to move suddenly and punish attackers, to 'bide one's time' until one can really be successful."

(Avedon 1971:418) Although they outline these structural elements in terms of physical actions, it is clear that taunting can function in the same way.

The complicated structure of the game of baseball results in a wide variety of skills that must be learned by its participants. The complexity of the game and the mastering of its skills are intrinsic motivations for its participants, just as the knowledge of the rules, the current statistics, and the league standings can be intrinsic motivations for the spectators as well as the players. It is not surprising, then, that almost the entirety of literature on sports speech, terms, nicknames, and sayings comes from the sport of baseball. Rule complexity also plays a role. According to Redl, Gump and Sutton-Smith, (Avedon 1971:412 The "pine tar" incident in 1983 involving George Brett of the Kansas City comes to mind) rule complexity can "increase demands on the comprehension of participants, enrich game experience, and cause unexpected advances and reversals". From the players' point of view, the overall effect of this interest in the inherent concerns of the game itself can effectively redirect the immediate concern with winning slightly to the point that the concentration is focused on the skills of the game. A batter who hits the ball very hard will still feel some sense of accomplishment even if the ball is caught. This is not to suggest that baseball players want to win any less than other athletes, but that the structure of the game demands that the concept of winning and losing be put in the perspective of a long season in which the statistical inevitability of losing serves to reassure the players that a particular loss is not overridingly threatening to the teams overall success. This is not true, for instance, in football since a football team plays only 16 games and one loss does indeed present a more significant setback to the team's overall success.[2]

Notice, then, the difference, in patterns of verbal expression in games that are structurally different. In football, each play is developed and practiced to perfection (hopefully), leaving little room for improvisation. Thus the tendency is to have certain dominant leader figures, such as the coach and the quarterback, who are essential in defining and executing the plays. Consequently, there are often severe restrictions on who is allowed to speak on the field since there is little time for discussion of anything other than strategic matters. Basketball represents the other end of the spectrum structurally, since, although there are set plays, the game is still played on a highly instinctive level. However, the most significant factor in its relative lack of folk speech is simply the fact that, because of its fast pace, there is little time to talk during the course of a game.

The structure of the game can also be an important factor in forming the psychological characteristics of the participants. Baseball players have a sense of humor about the game and themselves. In no other sport are there players who can exhibit their weaknesses so openly. (A recent beer advertisement featured baseball non-great Bob Uecker, with the caption "Great ballplayers drink Lite because it's less filling. I know. I asked one.") One reason for this apparent humility is that ballplayers are forced to exhibit their weaknesses openly when on the field. An error or strikeout happens out in the open for all of the players and spectators to see. These events also happen far enough away from the other players that there is no doubt who is at fault — there is no one else to blame. Furthermore, these mistakes are recorded for posterity along with all of the other statistics that are kept during games. If a guard in football misses a block on a running play, it may go unnoticed to a majority of the people watching the game (though probably not the coach). And the guard's error is not recorded in any official manner. In baseball there is no denying that a mistake happened. If a left fielder drops a fly ball, everyone — the players on both teams and the spectators — sees it happen. And, to add insult to injury, the error is recorded for all of time in the official statistics of the league. So such mistakes must simply be accepted. The players' ability to accept these mistakes lightheartedly (sometimes) is partly due to the fact that there are so many functions for a ballplayer to perform that he cannot always be expected to perform all with equal success. The pain of failure in one task may be alleviated by success in another. A shortstop may be known for his great fielding — his most important function — and so may be less sensitive about his poor hitting. (In contrast, think of a lineman in football. If he misses his block he has failed in his only duty.) One of the many functions a player can perform is to "loosen up" — mentally relax — the other players on his team by being funny. A player who is funny can not only lift his teammates spirits, but can do it at the expense of the opposition and thus become of strategic importance to his team. If a player is able to upset the opposition, it may be to the benefit of his team. So certain players are respected not only for their specific physical abilities, but also for their aptitude in verbal expression. The specification of skills and knowledge may carry over into the subject of intelligence in the larger scope of the players' knowledge of society in general and their attitude to other players' knowledge. A player who has a thorough knowledge of the strategic subtleties of the game may be alleviated of the condemnation of ignorance in worldly matters such as politics, literature, or music. It may be possible, then, that a player such as Yogi Berra, who is an intelligent ballplayer, is lifted of the onus of stupidity and is regarded as funny, rather than ignorant, when he comments on a popular restaurant that "Nobody goes there anymore. It's too crowded."

The environment in which baseball takes place further differentiates it from other sports.[3] In football and basketball, the fields conform to general specifications and the material composition of the field is usually homogeneous (grass for football, wood for basketball), whereas in baseball the variety of materials used in the separate elements (wood for fences, dirt for infield, canvas for bases, etc.) of the field, and the varying configurations of these elements, increase the number of idiosyncrasies in the relationship between the player and the field, and hence demand the need for players to "know" a particular field. That is, a player must know the particular aspects of each field that may affect the events of the game. For instance, a left fielder in Fenway Park in Boston must get used to how a baseball bounces off of the inordinately high wall — the "Green Monster" — in left field. The relationship between the player and the field is an important one. This encroachment of the field, of nature (baseball players often call the field "the park"), upon the game and the possibility of its influence on the outcome of game lends an air of cosmic involvement and suggests the uncontrollable influence of fate, luck, and nature on the game; think of Gabby Hartnett's "home run-in-the-dark" to put the Chicago Cubs in front of the Pittsburgh Pirates in the 1938 pennant race or the easy ground ball that hit a pebble and bounced past Fred Lindstrom to give Walter Johnson and his Washington Senators a victory over the New York Giants in the 1924 World Series. Indeed, many a game has been lost by a "bad hop", many a ball "lost in the sun". Such nature-related factors, in which defeat may be a result of bad luck rather than the direct influence of a human opponent, can tend to ease the pain of losing, thus creating a more amiable atmosphere and one that is sometimes amenable to conversation and joking. Of course, lest it be assumed that the suggestion is being made that there is a low degree of intensity among players, it should be mentioned that there are certain elements of the game that can result in a great deal of tension. The pressure to perform that is experienced by a batter with two outs on him in the bottom of the ninth inning, the bases loaded, his team losing by one run, and thousands of fans screaming at him may be unequaled in any other sport.

The field of play can also be related to the use of space as a cultural factor. In his famous work *Homo Ludens: A Study of the Play-Element in Culture,* Johan Huizinga notes the importance of the use of space in play and the significance of spatial relations that arise in our "playgrounds", the "temporary worlds within the ordinary world, dedicated to the performance of an act apart" which are "isolated, hedged round, hallowed, within which special rules obtain" (Huizinga 1949:10). It is important to realize, though, that the implications of these concepts, which are often applied to the study of childrens games, can be significantly different for adults. Thus, while the concept of the separateness of a playing field should be understood in this context, one should be careful in attempting to apply these statements as generalizations of the notion of the reference frame appropriate to adult activity. This was astutely elaborated upon by Erik Erikson in his book *Toys and Reasons, Stages in the Ritualization of Experience.* Erikson realizes that "the adult who is playing in a sphere set aside for 'play' is not comparable to a playing child; wherefore he often seems to be playing at playing." He notes, however, that "this in no way preempts the functions of a certain maturing playfulness which is endowed with adult competence, heightens the sense of reality, and enhances actuality in spheres of activity where facts are facts and acts count." (Erikson 1977:63). Thus there are important elements of play in the adult world, such as baseball, that must be regarded not as extensions of childrens play but as activities that retain the elements of playfulness itself, but in the sphere of adult activity. This is a crucial concept in examining baseball as a reflection of American society since it would be difficult, and incorrect, to categorize the adult players as just big children. Elements of both the adult world and the sphere of youthful play must be thought of as coexisting within the sport, just as they coexist in American society.

Chapter 3
THE AUDIENCE

An important concern for folklorists studying folk groups in performance is the question of who exactly is the audience. That is, it is important to determine who is watching, who is participating, and to what extent the audience is affecting the performance. The solution is not always that clear-cut. Sometimes those people watching are members of the folk group, sometimes they are not. Furthermore, some members of the group are participating to a greater extent than other members. The importance of these concerns lies in the fact that the audience can affect a folk group's performance. A sailor telling a joke in the presence of a clergyman may edit the joke in order to be less offensive, whereas the same joke told in front of his fellow sailors may retain more of its original, bawdy flavor. To the folklorist recording the telling of the joke, it is important to not only record both versions of the joke, but the audience for which each was told. The correlation of the data can then not only give information about each particular group, but also about the relationship between groups. This is important in the modern philosophy of folklore as a form of performance.

The folk group of baseball players presents an interesting case because the grouping of players is often very
clearly delineated and clear patterns of interaction are
often discernible. Furthermore, since the players are
separated from non-players during both games and practices, there is very little influence from anyone outside of the
folk group. The audience for the players' folk speech
consists almost entirely of the players themselves. Thus the
study of the grouping of players can provide both a
"microscopic" look at the game — the interactions between
players according to their functions and groupings — and a
"macroscopic" view of the entire group as a whole.
Conversation between teammates, as well as the taunting
of the opposition, happen, for the most part, on the field and
in (or from) the dugout and thus are not (usually) audible to
the spectators. Hence the audience for the players' folk
speech is composed of what Barre Toelken terms a "central
audience" (Toelken 1979:108) — an audience that is
composed solely of members of one folk group. Since both
the performers and listeners share the defining elements of
a particular folk culture, the cultural items of verbal
expression that are used are in what might be called a "pure
state". That is, they are not affected by the presence of an
outside audience that might change the general content of
the performance. The composition of this central audience
is particularly interesting. The collection of players on one
particular team comprise what is called an "esoteric"
audience. Esoteric applies to what a group thinks of itself,
as well as what it supposes others think of it.[1] Such beliefs
manifest in the form of verbal expression often arise from
the special knowledge that a group may possess. In this
context, their folk speech functions as a mechanism of
social cohesion. But the structure of the game involving the
competition between these teams involves an exoteric
dimension of the folk speech which results from tension
between groups. That is taunting acts as an instrument of
conflict and aggression between teams, even though it is
socially cohesive for teammates.[2] Thus baseball folk

speech convolves both the "disjunctive" effect of games and the "conjoining" brought about by ritual in Levi-Strauss' structuralist theory (Levi-Strauss 1966:32).

The knowledge of grouping and interaction between groups is useful in understanding the meaning and the function of the observed items of folk speech. Ultimately, however, function and meaning can only be determined through the understanding of the entire situation in which a particular item occurs; who said it, when they said it, and to whom they said it. A primary interest in this "rhetorical theory of folklore" is in the relationship between the speaker (the "performer") and the listener (the "audience"). The relationship between the performer and the audience is usually described in terms of the sympathetic response of the audience and often serves as a focal point in the construction of the theory of folklore as an element of social cohesion. However, the structure of the vocal performance in baseball demands a slight restructuring of this approach. A primary function of much of the verbal performance of insulting in baseball is the evocation of an antipathetic response from the members of the performer's group. This can result in an increase in tension between the performer (and his group), and the person to whom the insult is directed (and his group). The objective of the performer, in this case, is to alienate the listener. In other words, there is a sympathetic intragroup response, but an antipathetic intergroup response. Hence it is appropriate to differentiate between the general audience that hears the performance, and the audience to whom a particular item is specifically directed. In baseball, this latter audience is most often a single player. It is useful, then, to define such a player as a "target auditor". In general, a group of such auditors would make up a "target audience". The usefulness of such a concept is primarily in that it enables a more defined representation of the audience response. Since all members of an audience will not react similarly to an insult, it is important to try to delineate and categorize groups of

people that react in a particular manner. For instance, if a
hitter on team A is insulted by a player on team B, he may
feel a stronger sense of anger than may his teammates.
Furthermore, the players on team B may think the insult
was funny. If one is to accurately assess all possible affects
of such an insult, it is necessary to be able to have a way of
differentiating between the opposition in general and the
person on the opposition to whom the insult is actually
directed.

It is particularly interesting to consider how the level of
competition and the age of the players affects the use of
slang by the players. Since it is always important to keep in
mind the relationship between the audience and the
performer, it is necessary that changes in the content of the
folk speech in front of different audiences be noted. This can
reveal interesting information about the folk group in
question. In the previous discussion of audience, it was
mentioned that, in general, the players perform almost
exclusively among themselves, being spacially separated
from spectators and thus the spectators have virtually no
effect on the players' folk speech. However, this is not
necessarily true at the younger age levels. A great deal of
slang is suppressed at the level of high school baseball and
below because of the dominant role played by the coach. At
these levels, the coach is often a teacher or parent an
individual who is, at one time or another, responsible for the
social conduct of the players in a context outside of
baseball. This carries over into games and practices and the
result is the suppression of a great deal of taunting. At the
younger age levels, taunting is not viewed as "good
sportsmanship" mainly because it is not considered acceptable in a social context. The influence of the parent or
coach (as a leader figure) serves to promote idealistic
behavior, in theory at least. Thus any insult becomes an
expression of a violation of idealistic norms, since insulting
is considered rude in American culture, and so it is deterred.

As the level of competition and the age of the players increase and the sport becomes more removed from a social context, the collection of players evolves into a type of separate society. Consequently, it begins to develop its own concept of what is allowable. As a result, the coach's influence becomes limited strictly to aspects of the game. The coaches at the semi-pro level have little or no control over the players outside of games and practices. Yet, at the younger age levels, such as Little League, there is not such a well-defined baseball society and there can be a significant influence from the community in which a particular baseball team is located. This is pointed out in Gary Alan Fine's insightful study entitled "Small Groups and Culture Creation: The Idioculture of Little League Baseball Teams". He suggests that "teams do have different moral standards for propriety; this is due to their adult and child personnel, and the extent to which these personnel are willing to express their beliefs to shape public behavior." (Fine 1979:739) The point to be made is that at the advanced levels of competition individuals are not concerned with shaping public behavior — that is, altering standards of conduct — by the expression of their beliefs. At these levels, the baseball community itself becomes much more solidified and thus the norms of the players involve aspects of the game more than the norms of the society in which the team is embedded. At the most advanced levels of play, such as semi-professional and professional, very few cultural items (taunts, cant terms, etc.) are prohibited unless their content violates the norms of the baseball community itself. And because the norms of the baseball community concern primarily actions on the field rather than the subject matter of particular items of speech, very little is considered taboo when it comes to what the players may say. Among the Little League teams studied by Fine, though, it was noted that "members' personalities, religion, political ideology, or morality may influence the situational viability for a cultural item" (Fine 1979:739).

This shift in value structure from an emphasis on societal norms to those of the baseball community is evident not only in the players' speech, but in their actions and, more importantly, their attitudes towards these actions. For instance, at the advanced levels of competition, a flagrant transgression against baseball norms is a player stealing third base when his team is leading by a large margin. This is considered "rubbing it in" — embarassing the other team — because the "extra base" was not necessary from a strategic standpoint. It is not considered out of line, though, to ask an opposing pitcher who is having trouble getting batters out, "Where's your girl friend? There's a ballplayer missing!" which implies that the pitcher's girlfriend, who is presumably in attendance, has gotten bored and left with a player from the other team. Such sexual threats and implications of infidelity would most likely not be tolerated by a coach who was also a parent or teacher, as is often the case in Little League.

At the advanced levels, because the players are concerned primarily with the mores of the baseball community, there is less of an emphasis in their folk speech on religion, political ideology, and morality, among other things, that exist when the community outside of the team is involved. Instead, there is a concern with the game itself. The existence of vocal expressions resulting from the functional interactions of the game, the interaction of players at particular positions performing particular functions under specific circumstances, suggests that there would would exist ritual insulting in professional baseball very similar to that observed in semi-pro baseball. This idea was confirmed by informants who had played at the professional level.

It is particularly interesting to note that, despite the conscious effort to suppress taunting in the younger age levels of competition, the effects of slang still emerge as something of importance. In the very youngest leagues (ages about 7-10 years) it is common for the coach to yell to his defensive players, "Let's hear some chatter!". "Chatter" almost invariably means the players yelling "Hey, batter! Swing!" or simply "Hey, batter!" (Here the "hey" is drawn out.) These phrases are often repeated many times in succession for the simple purpose of disturbing the batter, thus serving the same purpose that taunting and insulting do in the older, more advanced leagues.

The fact that players at the younger age levels are less educated, both academically and socially, is also an important factor in the reduced amount of slang at these levels. But the significant lack of education is not necessarily academic, but in the ways of baseball. In the advanced levels of competition, In the advanced levels of competition, though an experienced player may not be well-read or possess an extensive vocabulary, he may have a good command of baseball language or know "the book" (information about a player's abilities) on opposing players. He may also keep close track of what is happening in the rest of the league. All of this gives the player confidence in his own intelligence, which can help improve his performance in games. Furthermore, such experienced ballplayers, or "veterans", can be respected members of the team because of their knowledge even though their physical talents may have diminished over the years. Their acquired knowledge can be an asset to the team and thus such a player can still hold the respect of other players — especially the younger players — even after his talent has left him.

Though baseball taunting is used in games primarily for strategic purposes, it is important in other ways during practice sessions. Taunting in practice can act as a substitute for the competitive aggression present in games and, because it is more good-natured, can have a unifying effect. It provides an indirect means of expressing affection, which is often a difficult task among American males.

Furthermore, by taunting each other in practice, players learn to take abuse. During games comments are made in a biting and caustic tone that projects disgust and derision. At the same time, a team's attitude towards the opposition is expected to be the oppositions's attitude towards them. The effect that a team wishes to provoke from the opposition is that which they themselves want to avoid. Hence, players must get used to hearing nasty and abusive comments directed towards them. Thus insulting may "serve as a dominant means of sustaining the kinds of character traits necessary for group survival" (Flynn 1977:10).

The grouping of players during practice is an important consideration. Because players are often grouped according to a common skill or function, the slang concerning that skill or function is intensified. Since a particular skill or function is emphasized in these groups, the folk speech of the participating group members becomes more focused. For instance, it is common for the pitchers to be grouped together to throw or the hitters to hit. The pitchers talk about pitching and the hitters talk about hitting. There becomes, in effect, a folk group substructuring within the larger structure of the team. For instance, often only one player can hit at a time. The other members of this subgroup (i.e., the other hitters) are confined to observation. This, in turn, leads to conversation, often centered around the person who is active and the skill that he is practicing. This has the effect of concentrating the slang concerning that position or skill; in this case, hitting. Since often only one player may perform at a time, while the other players watch him, such vocal expression can increase his intensity, since he performing in from of his peers. This may have the effect of enhancing the effectiveness of his training in the particular skill that he is practicing. Insulting within these "position sub-groups" can also serve as a means by which people who are often competing to play can, by increasing the frequency of interaction, suppress conflict (Coser 1956:152). Such organ-ization acts as a strong affirmation of group structure among the "position" groups and reasserts their solidarity. This reflects Freud's theory of group tolerance in which "so long as a group formation persists or so far as it extends, individuals in the group behave as though they were uniform, tolerate the peculiarities of its other members, equate themselves with them, and have not feelings of aversion toward them." (Freud 1960:43) One would suspect that this concept might also be important among the infielders, who have to work closely as a cooperative unit in order for the team to be effective defensively.

An interesting element of practices is the games that the players play to warm up. These games are often not extremely competitive, but are primarily for the purpose of emphasizing a particular skill and often do not have any "winner". Consequently, the games provide a level of intensity low enough to avoid excessive tension but high enough to stimulate a high degree of participant impulse expression. The mood is then often one of jovial and energetic enthusiasm. An example of such a game is "flip". In the game of "flip" a player with a bat faces about 5 or 6 fielders at a distance of about twenty feet. The ball is thrown to the batter, who hits it back on the ground to the fielders. (If it is hit in the air, the player who catches it becomes the hitter.) When a fielder gets the ball, he flips the ball with his glove to another fielder who, in turn, flips it to another, and so on. This continues until all players have touched the ball once and only once. The object of the game for the fielders is to avoid making any fielding mistakes. For the batters, it is important to develop good enough control of the bat to consistently hit the ball solidly and on the ground. Since a fielding error sends a player to the end of the line, a player who does not err will eventually end up at the front of the line where he becomes the player designated to become the hitter when and if the current hitter makes a hitting error. There are many rules concerning "legal" ways to flip the ball; how hard it can be flipped, how one can fake, etc. (These rules often vary from team to team.) The judgement of fault is left to the batter and thus he becomes the target of much (good-natured) abuse. Besides being fun, the game is a good way to both reacquaint players at the beginning of practices (or games) as well as get them in an aggressive mood and ready for weightier matters. Players enjoy playing it as well as watching teammates play it. Teammates who are not participating in the game but are just watching often join in the taunting of the players in the game. Such games provide the perfect atmosphere for the use of taunting as a cohesive social force.

Chapter 4

UNDERSTANDING FOLK RHETORICAL STRATEGY

In studying the folk speech of any group, it is important to consider not only what is said, but how and why it is said. That is, it is important to understand folk rhetorical strategy. One of the main problems with folklore studies in the past, and one that is still surprisingly common today, is the emphasis on simply the collection of data. Folklorists will often collect scores of examples of a certain proverb or saying, for instance, without ever addressing the fundamental question of what they mean. To be sure, the collection of data is a necessary element in the process of folklore studies, yet it must exist as a supplement to the task of interpretation. Ultimately, the function of an item of folklore, the reason for its existence, can only be found through the discovery of its meaning. Consequently, it is essential that the context of an item be noted. Recording not only a particular item of folklore, but the context in which it arises, is essential to the study of what Richard Bauman calls the "social nature of folklore performance," a subject whose understanding is vital to correct interpretation of folklore. The neglect of this concept has been one of the major failures of writings on baseball folk speech. Almost the entire corpus of work done on baseball folk speech has focused on cant terms, which are primarily a form of artistic verbal *communication* (Bauman 1971:39-41). But in neglecting the insulting rituals in baseball, the bulk of the artistic verbal *performance* in baseball has been overlooked.

Simply put, artistic verbal communication is a method of transmitting information. Communicative interaction between the performer and the audience requires that there be a mutually held knowledge of the esthetic conventions of the method of expression that is to be employed. Artistic verbal performance transcends the mere communication of information, entering into a domain in which the esthetic value of an item within a particular context is of primary importance. The explanation of artistic verbal performance offered by Bauman is a succinct presentation of the factors that must be understood when analyzing this phenomenon:

"By artistic use of spoken language, artistic verbal performance, is meant language usage which takes on special significance above and beyond its referential, informational dimension through the systematic elaboration of any component of verbal behavior in such a way that this component calls attention to itself and is perceived as uncommon or special in a particular context. It may validly be argued that all speech has an esthetic dimension, but it is the point at which awareness of the esthetic dimension is achieved, at which the esthetic is invoked and the speech is intended or recognized as special, which holds the key to artistic verbal performance and responses thereto." (Bauman 1971:39)

Players' awareness of the esthetic dimension of a great deal of their folk expressions is itself influential in the structure of verbal interaction among players and this is precisely the defining element of verbal performance. As in any other form of social behavior, artistic verbal performance is influenced by a variety of cultural factors. It is important when analyzing a particular item to ask how the performer perceives the entirety of the situation in which his performance takes place. This must include an understanding of both the physical and psychic aspects within a particular time frame, the overall structure of the culture in which he is situated, the audience, and what it is that he wants to achieve. All of this must be taken into account along with the performer's actual or potential relationship with the audience.

Almost all of the previous literature on baseball folk speech has focused on "cant" terms. The difficulty with taking this approach is that it implies that the whole of baseball folk speech is an attempt at formulating an oral structure of merely descriptive elements. This ignores the importance of the human factors of the sport: the players and their interactions. In accepting this approach, one eliminates the importance of the concept of a "team". In fact, the dynamics of all the group structures that exist in the game are neglected. Consequently, all of the competition between teams, which is the primary motivation behind taunting, is neglected and, along with it, the greater part of baseball folk speech. Yet even the terms and short phrases that are studied often suffer in interpretation because of the neglect of context.

Take, for example, the phrase "waste a pitch" or "waste one". The definition of this offered by Eric Partridge in *Slang — Today and Yesterday* is "to pitch a ball so high or far outside that the batsman cannot reach it" (Partridge 1933:317). This definition has some element of truth to it, yet it is far too broad to explain what the term means and when it is said. The real meaning of this phrase cannot be understood unless it is discussed within the context of the situation in which it is most often said. The situation in question is almost invariably when the "count" on the batter is no balls and two strikes. Here the pitcher is at an advantage and is said to be "way ahead" of the batter.

Since the batter is in danger of "striking out", he must be especially alert. A batter can often become anxious in this situation and be somewhat less selective of pitches in order to avoid being "called out on strikes" — letting a third strike go by without swinging at it. A pitcher can capitalize on this situation by throwing a pitch just out of the strike zone; close enough to look good, but far enough away to be difficult to hit. Though the pitcher is usually concerned with throwing strikes, in this situation he is afforded the luxury of being able to "waste a pitch". Thus the phrase carries the implication of the pitchers intent of throwing a "ball".

Further mishandling of this term is seen in *Baseball Wit and Wisdom* by Frank Graham and Dick Hyman, who offer that "waste one" is "a pitcher who deliberately throws outside the strike zone" (Hyman 1962:244). Besides leaving the obvious question — "Why does the pitcher want to throw the ball outside the strike zone?" — unanswered, it is unlikely that Graham and Hyman intend to imply what their grammatical construction suggests — that "waste one" is "a pitcher". Again, the primary problem has been the neglect of context.

These problems have arisen, presumably, because the collector, as audience, has neglected the idea of Dan Ben-Amos, expressed in his article "Towards a Definition of Folklore in Context", that "For the folkloric act to happen, two social conditions are necessary: both performers and the audience have to be in the same situation and be part of the same reference group" (Ben-Amos 1971:12). Evidently, this is not usually the case. Data is rarely collected in the "dugout" during games. This has inevitably led to such statements as "Certainly there is no such thing as the folk speech of baseball players" (Coffin 1971:51).[1]

Since a great deal of baseball folk speech originates in response to specific social or strategic situations, it is important to think of the baseball community as dynamic, rather than static. The sociological theory of symbolic interactionism (Blumer 1969) is well suited for such a purpose, as it proposes that "cultural norms, status positions, and role relationships are only frameworks in which that process of formative transaction goes on" (Blumer, quoted in Buckley 1967:21). The purpose of baseball slang is not a singular one and the knowledge of the grouping of the players is imperative to the study and interpretation of the usage and meaning of the particular items of the players' folk speech since a great deal, especially taunting, is created in response to tensions existing in or between group structures. Taunting the opposition can have the effect of disturbing them to the point that it hinders their performance. An early study by psychologist D.A. Laird (Laird 1923) showed evidence that "razzing" could inhibit performance on simple motor coordination functions.[2] Of course, baseball folk speech is also used simply because of "the pleasure of using it, the prestige which comes from deft familiarity, the sense of belonging to the group, the ease with which it expresses moods and emotions, and the fun of rolling it off the tongue." (Maurer 1945:908), gratifications that David Maurer recognized in his analysis of military slang.

As would be expected, there is also taunting among players on the same team. Such intragroup taunting can be supportive to the team structure in a sport dominated by individuals. That is, it is a method of defining representative roles which, in turn, "set a normative limit to the pursuit of self-interest in a social system which is pervaded by an ethos of individual success" (Coser 1956:114-115). Each player performs as an individual, yet must ultimately act collectively with his teammates. Taunting among teammates can serve as a means by which players are reminded of their equality within the team structure. At the heart of this social bonding and the balance that is achieved, through verbal expression, between the associative force of the team structure and the dissociative element in the conflict between individual personalities that arises through verbal expression is the "sympathetic activity" that Roger Abrahams delineates as the mediating force in the building of community (Abrahams 1968:148). Performance can evoke a sympathetic response from the audience and reaffirm the community of the audience.

When directed towards the opposition, taunting forms a cohesive voice of the team and increases the players' concept of themselves as a team. From a social point of view, the need for cohesion is possibly influenced by the players' lack of familiarity with one another, since the players on a team usually are not selected by social factors, but are often grouped as such by geographical considerations or according to their talents. They must form a social group once they are brought together to form a team. On a larger scale, the specialized language of the sport gives the players on both teams a common sense of identity as members of the baseball community. The emphasis on the importance of the social microcosm leads to the framework of symbolic interactionism theory, in which "the microcosm of face-to-face interaction, including insult behavior, defines, supports, and maintains the macrocosm of the sociocultural order" (Flynn 1977:3). The basis of the process of formative transaction is rooted in the role relationships of the players and the cultural norms of the baseball community. Since baseball teams can differ greatly in terms of baseball culture in general, one might surmise that teams may be considered to be separate folk groups, and, indeed, there are particular aspects of baseball folk speech that vary from team to team.

Taunting can play an important role in the psychology of the team as a whole. In his early work, *Psychologie des Foules,* psychoanalyst G. Le Bon pointed out that there is a lowering of the intellectual ability of the individual when he becomes merged with a group, and thus there is an inhibition of the collective intellectual functioning of the group. Certainly a game as complex as baseball requires a good deal of mental capability and thus its players unconsciously seek a method of negating the mental anesthesia produced by the group (the team). The way in which this is achieved is best understood by W. McDougall's five "principal conditions" for raising the collective mental ability of a group to a higher level (from Freud 1960:24). His first condition is the manifestation of some degree of continuity of existence in the group. This condition is met because of the existence of teams and leagues, whose persistence results in the desired representation of continuity. The second condition is the definite idea of the individual in the group of the "nature, composition, functions, and capacities" of the group (so that he may develop an emotional relationship to the group). The third condition is the interaction (possibly rivalrous) with groups similar but distinct. This condition is satisfied by the competition between teams. The fourth condition is the possession of traditions, customs, and habits — "especially such as determine the relations of its members to one another". And the fifth condition is the existence of a definite structure of the group revealed in the specialization and differentiation of the functions of the individuals of the group. This condition is satisfied by the existence of player positions on the teams. The importance of the players' folk speech arises in the second and fourth requirements, as it is through traditional vocal expression that players are able to determine their relationships to each other as well as realize the nature and capacity of the group.

Attention to the grouping of players and the structure of these groups is essential to the study of baseball folk speech. It is essential to study the folk rhetorical strategy involved in baseball folk speech, especially taunting, within the context of social interaction, with particular attention to group dynamics. The primary functions of baseball folk speech result from the competition between various group structures; most notably, between teams. Affective group structures exist not only in the obvious form of teams but in smaller, less discrete groups within teams, especially according to position. With this in mind, the function of baseball speech can be understood by the analysis of specific situations that occur during games. Since certain specific situations arise regularly at the different positions, it is essential when discussing a particular item that the speaker, the person to whom the comment is said, and the situation in which the comment is used, be noted if one is to extract any meaning, and from the meaning, the function. This sensitivity to context becomes essential then, for, as Dundes states, "Function is essentially an abstraction made on the basis of a number of contexts" (Dundes 1978:27).

One of the ultimate goals when studying the folk speech of a group is, of course, to determine the purpose that the verbal expressions serve. The primary purpose of baseball taunts, as they arise during game situations, is to upset the opposition by breaking their concentration and, in doing so, hinder their performance. It is important to realize that taunting can serve a very real purpose in games. If individuals on a team have their concentration and confidence upset by the taunts of the opposition, they are much more likely to perform ineffectively. Vocal aggression is another channel to assert power against the opponent. While Abrahams' notion that the power of control over a problem situation exists in the objectification of the situation (Abrahams 1971:19) is applicable within the context of the sympathetic response of the esoteric structure of a particular team — that is, between players on the same team, taunting the opposition can function in the opposite manner, psychologically reducing the control of the person being insulted. Taunting an opponent who has made an error asserts the vocal aggressor's control through the antipathetic response emanating from the exoteric dimension of the intergroup structure by projecting the individual experience into an antagonistic domain, enhancing the individual's anxiety.

The function of insult in baseball is in some ways similar to that of insulting rituals such as the "signifying" of black ghetto youths[3] in which a person uses insults to "manipulate and control people and situations to give himself a winning edge" (Burling 1970:158). Yet there are critical distinctions to be made. In contrast to the structural aspect of the response patterns in signifying,[4] baseball taunts are not answered. Though taunts are primarily directed towards individuals, the insulted player (the target auditor) must not answer since his distraction would hinder his play and acknowledge the achievement of the opponents' goal — the disruption of his concentration. Thus insensitivity to insult is a necessary attribute of a baseball player. A player who becomes noticeably upset by the opposition's remarks will be taunted even further for his sensitivity, since the ability to take verbal abuse is a norm of the baseball society; its neglect is an admission of mental defeat and is thus a distasteful act. The individual's "answer" is left to his physical performance.

If a player (or possibly an umpire) becomes noticeably upset by the opposition's taunts, he is likely to hear something to the effect that he possesses "rabbit ears" — ears that hear everything. The actual implication is that the player reacts to everything he hears. The term "rabbit ears" has fallen somewhat from favor among ballplayers because of its widespread usage. It has given way to comments such as "Tuck in your ears!" and "Have a carrot!", both of which refer to characteristics of rabbits; they eat carrots and they have long ears, which would undoubtedly have to be tucked under baseball caps were they to wear them. Notice that both of these terms cannot be understood without previous knowledge of the term "rabbit ears". This type of development of slang is not uncommon among baseball players and will be termed "second order" slang. In this vein, the expression from which the second order term derives — in this case "rabbit ears" — can be called the "primary" term. Note that both of the second order comments have transformed the primary comment into a command. Since a command emphasizes the superiority of the speaker, the transformation yields a more effective taunt. Furthermore, comments that have become very common are revitalized as slang expressions by the development of second order terms, which serve to sustain the idea promoted by the primary term, while the variation in wording enforces the concept of a "slang" term. Shakespeare readers will recall a similar use of such indirection in insulting in *Twelfth Night* which Maria, the servant, says to the puritanical Malvolio, "Go shake your ears!", implying that he is an ass.

The necessity of remaining unaffected by insult reflects the importance the players put on the trait of toughness. This conscious restraint is a quality necessary for success in the game. It is this trait, acquired through participation in sport, that Konrad Lorenz sees as one of the great values of sport; "The value of sport, however, is much greater than that of a simple outlet of aggression in its coarser and more individualistic behavior fighting patterns. It educates a man to a conscious and responsible control of his own fighting behavior. More educational still is the restriction imposed by the demands for fairness and chivalry which must be respected even in the face of the strongest aggression-eliciting stimuli." (Lorenz 1966) Another good example of this attitude of baseball players is exhibited towards a player who complains excessively. Most often this occurs when a player (usually a pitcher) complains vehemently to an umpire over a call. If the player persists loudly in his debate, he is likely to hear "Waaa! Cry me a river!" (Here "Waaa!" is similar to the sound of a baby crying.) The implication is that the player is not tough enough to handle the small defeats that occur during the course of a game and is thus a "crybaby". Similar implications exist in "Want your milk bottle?!" (Frank 1926:41).

The burden of an insult, then, is shifted from the individual to the team as "any insult against a member of a kin group is regarded as an affront to the entire group; moreover, responding to an insult is not merely the duty of the particular individual who was the direct object of the insult, but of the entire family" (Flynn 1977:30). Furthermore, the response of the team can enhance the players' idea of themselves as a team. Teammates respond only when the actions of the opponent dictate insult and thus the meanings of particular comments are very dependent upon situation. This "situational" quality of baseball folk speech is the motivation for the organization of this analysis into sections focusing on certain positions, since situations occur most often according to position. The focus is on what will be called the four basic groups: the umpires, the fielders, the hitters, and the pitchers.

The existence of representational roles is important in the organization of insults by players but it does not preclude the existence of a complex tension arising from the conflict between the individual as personality and the individual as role type in game situations. Both the ritual and dramatic action in the game is structurally similar, or at least functionally equivalent, to the process of verbal dueling. Thus it is important to consider the psychological implications of the underlying symbolism. The psychoanalytic significance of much of the folk speech arises largely from the agonistic structure of interaction existing within the context of an all-male sport. From this arises a significant undercurrent of sexual symbolism. Importantly, these psychoanalytic patterns still reflect the structure of the functional grouping inherent in the game (the so-called four basic groups) and thus it is possible to reconcile the underlying symbolism with the specific role representations and status positions. There arises, then, a symbolic pattern in the insulting that reflects the struggle for power between the pitcher and the hitter, the defensive nature of the fielders and their need for dexterity, and the ruling power and necessary objectivity of the umpires.

The situational nature of taunts serves as a reflection of each particular conflict situation. As Kenneth Burke, in his appraisal of "self-consciously voiced expression", states, "These strategies size up the situations, name their structure and outstanding ingredients, and name them in a way that contains an attitude towards them" (Burke 1961:3). According to the rhetorical theory supported by Burke, verbal expression is a method of gaining control over a situation because it allows that situation to be delineated. To be able to denominate a situation is to know it, and to know it is to have some degree of control over it. The individual effort of verbal expression reaffirms the power of the individual, lending the performance a dimension of self-consciousness. The strategy, or method of encompassing the situation, is therefore dependent upon the individual's knowledge of the esthetic elements of strategy common to both himself and the culture in which he is performing. In order for the performance to be affective, these elements must be shared by both the performer and the audience.

Situations change very quickly in baseball games and there is often a shift in emotional momentum from one team to another. Players are very astute at sensing when the opposition is in trouble and thus most vulnerable to derision. Taunting is done in the hopes of using the instability of a player's situation to further his frustration and is often witty as "wit asserts itself in an aggressive — often contest — situation in which anxiety is a natural concomitant." (Dundes 1975:193). Wit can also serve as an outlet for the expression of subjects considered taboo in a particular society. At the same time, it gives a boost to the ego of the speaker, as pointed out by Sigmund Freud in his book *Jokes and their Relation to the Unconscious* (Freud 1960). Thus taunting can enhance the confidence of the speaker.

A player who is performing poorly is more likely to be taunted than one who is doing well. This is part of the attempt to break the confidence of the other team during games, where the opponent is continually derided or "rided" [hence the term "bench jockey" for the derider (Frank 1941:18-19)] in order to break their concentration and confidence. If a team is able to upset the other team, they will have a distinct advantage. Thus slang can play an important role in games. Though insults are usually directed at individuals, it is not uncommon to hear players insult an entire team. Such is the case when a defensive team is doing poorly "in the field". This may prompt the offensive team to suggest that the defensive team's collective abilities are little more than humorous entertainment and they should "Pitch a tent over that circus!". This same idea is implied in the comment "Who's your manager? Barnum and Bailey?!", the manager being the head coach of the team.

Chapter 5
FORMULAIC STRUCTURING

Possibly one of the strongest verifications of the concept of baseball players as a folk group is the existence of formulaic slang — comments which have set sentence structures, or "formulae", whose recognized form is useful in quickly evoking a particular idea. In doing so, the speaker is given a standard formal structure with known connotation within which to formulate either a standard or original image or concept. The stylistic structuring of formulaic expressions is a presentation of control by the speaker. By being able to comment on a situation in a traditionally recognizable form, the speaker is not only able to project the conflict of the situation into the domain of the audience, but is also able to resolve it because he is able to grasp the situation, understand it, as well as use it to his advantage. At the same time, the rhetorical nature of formulaic expressions also asserts the power of the speaker, amplifying his role as a performer rather than his status as an individual player. Consequently, the performer gains respect as an individual who can function efficiently, as a member of his own group, within the conflicting intergroup structure created by the competition between groups.

One common formula is of the form "Mix in a Y!". This construction is used in a variety of situations to suggest the inclusion of the object or concept Y. For instance, a coach may tell a pitcher to "Mix in a curveball!" as a suggestion to throw more curves. The object to be "mixed in" is always stated in the singular, though the implication is often for more than one to be included. This construction is often given a sarcastic tone and thus becomes a means of derision rather than advice. One of the most commonly heard examples of this type of usage arises when a pitcher has thrown an inordinate amount of balls and has "walked" a lot of batters. Someone on the opposition will often yell "Mix in a strike!" Also common is "Mix in a hit!" which is said to a batter who is hitless. In general, the "Mix in a Y" construction is used in a wide variety of situations, functioning on the basic assumption that the speaker is suggesting the inclusion of something that is lacking.

The most interesting and imaginative formula used in baseball folk speech is "I've seen better A in a B!" This formula is used in order to chastise the opponent for their errors or to suggest a lack of ability. It is based primarily on the use of a colloquial term or a homonym of a baseball term (usually metonymous) in space A. Space B is then the location of the nounal homonym of the term in space A. The term in B is most often an inanimate object, which enhances the notion of inaction and ineffectiveness. This is evident in the comment "I've seen better arms on a chair!" which is yelled by an offensive player to someone on the defense who has made a poor throw. There is no proposed relationship between a chair and the player; the force of the comment is in the opposition of the action that the player performs (throwing) and the inanimation of the object (the chair), the implication being that the player's "arm" (his ability to throw) is poor. The structural aspect of these comments acts as a logical structuring of concepts that supports the notion of Dundes that "it is certainly possible that much American logic and reassuring is closely tied to

metaphor in general and to visual metaphor in particular"
(Dundes 1980:86), as the comparison between A and B is
based on the speaker's sight.

It is common for there to be more than one construction
around the same word in space A. For instance the previous
example is closely related to "I've seen better arms on a
clock!". Sometimes changes are centered around the term in
space B. This last comment is similar to the comment said
to a player who has made a fielding error; "I've seen better
hands on a clock!", where the metonymous usage of
"hands" refers to the ability to field. It often becomes a
matter of interest for players to invent new forms of term B
relating to a particular term A. Another frequently used
comment of this form is saved for a player who has made a
mental mistake, such as throwing the ball to the wrong
base. An outfielder who tried to throw out a runner from
third base at home plate on a base hit, letting the batter who
got the hit go to second base and, of course, allowing the
runner on third to score, might hear someone on the the
opposition tell him "I've seen better heads on a lettuce!"
where "head" refers to the player's ability to think. The
implication is that the outfielder is somewhat lacking in
intelligence. Another example involves a player who is not
able to judge the position of the ball well when batting (i.e.,
does not have a "good eye"). He may hear "I've seen better
eyes on a potato!" The use of objects such as potatoes is
possibly a reflection of the rural influence in baseball.
Constructions in which term A is an action include "I've
seen better swings in a park!" where swing refers to a
batter's swing of his bat. Sometimes the actions in space B
include sexual themes. These comments may have a
twofold implication; the player to whom the comment is
said is seen to be not only deficient in baseball talent, but
also in sexual ability. Such is the case when players are
taunting a pitcher on the opposition for his "move". A
"move" in baseball terminology is the pitcher's motion to
try to "pick off" a runner catch him standing off of the base

(and thus is in danger of being tagged out). The pitcher may be told "I've seen better moves in a drive-in!", "I've seen better moves in a cheap hotel", or "I've seen better moves in an orgy". The homonymic form of "moves" refers to movements during sexual activities. Hence the speaker is one who can discriminate between good and bad "moves". That is, he has a knowledge of sexual expertise. By expressing his sexual knowledge, and implied sexual prowess, the speaker presents himself as a sexual threat to his opponent.

Examples of this formula in which term A is a slang term include "I've seen better hoses in a garden!" where hose is a slang term that is equivalent to "arm" in meaning. Also included in this catagory is "I've seen better cuts in a deli!" in which "cut" refers to a batter's swing. Aside from being antagonistic, the use of these taunts concerning the mundane materials and objects of everyday life such as hoses, gardens, and delicatessens, functions within Lewis Coser's definition of "group consciousness" in which there is (Coser 1956:115) "the transformation of individuals with their own specific life situations into conscious representatives of the group." That is, this is one way in which the structure of verbal expression in the game of baseball enhances the notion of the individuals in that community as members of a truly separate society by presenting elements of the outside world within the context of situations peculiar to the baseball community.

An important point to notice in this particular formula, "I've seen better A in a B!", is the position of the speaker as a figure of experience and knowledge. When the speaker says, "I've seen ..." he implies that he has previous knowledge of the actions upon which he is commenting, supporting Dundes' idea that (Dundes 1980:87) "American speech provides persuasive evidence to support the notion that 'vision' is used as a metaphor for 'understanding'." The performer is one who understands the situation that he sees. This asserts his control over the situation. Furthermore, the speaker is one who has traveled, having seen gardens, drive-ins, delis, cheap hotels, and orgies. Traveling is an integral part of baseball, though it is often not the most enjoyable aspect of the game. The traveling implied in these comments highlights the fact that the speaker has put in a lot of time traveling, has acquired a lot of "hands-on" knowledge, and deserves the respect due an experienced veteran player.

Another common formula is "X, then pop off!" To "pop off" is to talk boldly or to complain. This construction may be used in response to the complaints (usually those directed to an umpire) of an opponent. For instance, if a pitcher has failed to get an out in a particular inning and is complaining loudly to the umpire about a call, an opposing player may tell the pitcher to "Get an out, then pop off!" The implication is that the pitcher has no business complaining as the unfortunate situation in which he finds himself is his own fault and that in arguing with the umpire he is merely venting his own frustration. The idea being expressed by the speaker is similar to that implicit in the idea of toughness that is so much a part of the baseball players' philosophy. Both the physical pains and the mental setbacks suffered in the game are to be accepted. This same construction may also be used as a retort to a suggestion of the inadequacy of the speaker. If, for instance, player A (who is hitless that day) is good-naturedly chastising teammate B for, say, committing an error in the field the previous inning, player B may respond, in a slightly sharper tone, "Get a hit, then pop off!" The context of this construction as a rebuff to verbal assault serves to create an emotional reversal that tends to quell the antics of a verbal aggressor. Hence it can be used simply to quiet an overzealous or obnoxious person. Thus it is useful in the taunting of a fan who is insulting players during a game. If the fan is fat, for instance, a player may tell him to "Lose some weight, then pop off!".

Another fairly common construction is "X all of Y." The non-specific nature of the word "all", when used sarcastically, serves to highlight the insignificant or inappreciable quality of Y. For instance, when describing an opponents home run that barely cleared the outfield fence that is, say, 310 feet away, a player may say "It went all of 310 feet." This implies that the hit was not very impressive. Of course, it does not matter by how far the ball cleared the fence — it was still a home run. Yet this comment has a way of trivializing the achievement of the opponent. The generality of this comment results in its use in many situations that do not involve aspects of the game. A fairly common social situation for the use of this construction occurs when a pretty young girl walks by a group of players, one of whom seems to be taking particular interest in the spectacle. A fellow observer may say to him, "She's all of fifteen years old!", implying that the girl is too young for him.

Some formulaic constructions are merely descriptive. For instance, a particular construction that is used to denote that something is good or "professional" is "Major League X." "Major League" refers to the top level of professional baseball and thus represents the paradigm of baseball prowess. For instance, in the non-professional leagues, a ball that is hit inordinately high in the outfield is often called a "Major League fly ball". That is, it was hit as high as a Major League ballplayer might a fly ball. This construction is used in the lower levels of competition as well as in the professional ranks (Bouton 1970:123) and it has become fairly common in American speech as a synonym for a top level of quality or achievement. In Howard Hawkes' film "Ball of Fire" (Hawkes 1941), starring Gary Cooper and Barbara Stanwyck, Miss Stanwyck, on being presented with an engagement ring (which has quite a large diamond in it), calls it a "Major League ring".[1]

There are other formulae that are used with some degree of regularity. Most of them, though, are not as particular to baseball, and are more representative of the folk speech of American youths. For example, "X city" is a construction that is common among adolescents and college students as well as baseball players. It is used to emphasize the abundance or inevitability of X. It may be said of a high scoring game that it was "home run city", if a lot of home runs were hit. Similarly, it may be predicted that a game in which a particularly ineffective pitcher is scheduled to face a hard-hitting team will be "home run city". Also common in these same folk groups is "X me!", which is used as a request that someone give the speaker an object X, as in "Beer me!" (i.e., "Give me a beer!"). This is also commmonly heard in colleges, as is the widely used "Nice X!", which is said in a sarcastic tone and hence implies that the object of the verb is not nice or good but bad or defective in some way. Any object or action that does not meet the approval of the speaker may be prefixed with "nice" in order to denote its inadequecy. For instance, a player who is overweight or very thin may hear "Nice body!", implying that he does not have an aesthetically pleasing or a functional body. A player who exhibits poor judgement might hear "Nice mind!", suggesting that he possesses a minimal amount of intelligence and should try to "Have an idea out there!" (i.e., think). These comments can also be metonymous, as in "Nice glove!", suggesting the defensive inadequacies of a player who makes an error in the field.

Though the similarity in certain aspects of the folk speech of baseball players and American youth in general is probably a carry-over from the players' younger days — if they are, in fact, not still young — it has been argued by some that sports itself perpetuates adolescence, thus implying, in effect, that it would perpetuate adolescent verbal patterns. Johan Huizinga, in his analysis of modern society *In The Shadow of Tomorrow: A Diagnosis of the Spiritual Ills of Our Time* speaks of (Huizinga 1936:217) "the attitude of a community whose behavior ... instead of making the boy into the man adapts its conduct to that of the adolescent age." However, the continuance of such conduct in baseball is much more likely to be the result of the structure of the game itself, in which personal interaction leads to verbal expression that itself plays a role similar to that which it plays for adolescents in their years of formative social interaction; primarily, the control over conflict situations.

Chapter 6
A NOTE ON PROFANITY

Profanity is an integral part of baseball players' folk speech and its subtleties deserve as much scrutiny as any other aspect of their folklore. It is often neglected, however; possibly because of its potentially offensive nature. Interestingly, the use of profanity has become, in some instances, almost as specific as the situational nature of many taunts. Because profanity can be somewhat offensive in nature, people often neglect the fact that it can function as more than just an expletive. Profane terms and phrases can have specific meanings and serve specific functions.

Consider the distinction that has arisen among the terms "bullshit", "horseshit", and "chickenshit". Though these words seem to possess a variety of meanings in the folk speech of other folk groups, they have become well defined in the realm of baseball folk speech. The basic distinctions are that "bullshit" means "not true", "horseshit" means "bad" or "low class", and "chickenshit" means "gutless" (i.e., afraid). Further, "bullshit" is often used as a retort, or as an immediate reaction to an event. It is of a slightly stronger sense than the other two and thus often said in a harsher tone. "Horseshit" is of a lesser degree accusative and often simply descriptive. Hence it is applicable in many more circumstances than "bullshit". "Chickenshit" is the most specific of the three terms and is thus applicable in fewer situations.

Because of the accusative nature of the word "bullshit", it is not surprising that it is often directed towards umpires. A player disagreeing with an umpire's call may yell "Bullshit, ump!". The player feels that the call was wrong or "bullshit". However, when describing the call , he is likely to say, "It was a horseshit call." That is, it was a bad call. That player feels that it was a "horseshit" (bad) call because it was "bullshit" (wrong). "Bullshit" can also carry the implication of lying. A player who deems an umpire's call "bullshit" is, in some sense, implying that the umpire is lying. This is consistent with the tendency of players to suggest that an umpire is lying in order to give the other team an advantage.

The equivalence of the word "horseshit" with "bad" or "low class" leads to a plethora of possible uses. It has become one of the most popular words among baseball players, possibly because of the versatile nature of the word inherent with its synonymity with "bad"[1] It is of great utility to ballplayers because its meaning is specific enough to be readily recognized and, at the same time, it fulfills the act of swearing which (Montague 1967:794) "functions as a form of relief for sudden surges of hostile or aggressive behaviour that require appropriate channels for expression." A wonderful example of the concision that this term affords is evident in a ballplayer's less than favorable description of Cincinnati, Ohio (Bouton 1970:362); "Horseshit park, horseshit clubhouse, horseshit hotel, lots of movies, nice place to eat after the game, tough town to get laid in." Another very common term synonymous with "bad" is "brutal", which is usually used to denote a lack of talent, luck, or goodness. A player with poor fielding ability is said to be "brutal in the field" (on defense), a ball that takes a bad hop is said to "take a brutal bounce" (conveying

the bad luck of the intended fielder), and a player who has
had a bad day is said to have had a "brutal game".

The most specific of the three terms is "chickenshit". It
is usually used as an adverb and is synonymous with
"unnecessary" or "gutless", implying that a particular
action is unfair or unnecessarily dangerous. The implication of "gutless" is that a particularly drastic measure was
taken because the perpetrator lacked the skill to accomplish
the action within the rules of the game. For instance,
"spiking" a player (gouging him with the metal "cleats" on
the bottom of baseball shoes) is considered "chickenshit"
because it unnecessarily endangers a player. If, however, a
runner heading toward second base knocks down ("takes
out") the shortstop in an effort to force an error, the action is
considered appropriate as a necessary attempt to avoid a
double play. Roughness is not necessarily a factor, then, as
long as it exists within the sphere of "fair" behavior. For a
pitcher to throw at a batter's chin in order to intimidate him
is perfectly acceptable. But to throw behind a hitter's head
for the same purpose is not. Since a hitter's natural reaction
to a ball thrown near his head is to back up, he is likely to
involuntarily back directly into a pitch thrown at his head.
To throw behind a player's head on purpose reveals an
intention to injure the player, which is not acceptable. It is
"chickenshit".

It is interesting to consider why a particular animal is
used in the above comments. Certainly this would be
difficult, if not impossible, to determine precisely. The
region of the country in which the term is used, the situation
in which it is employed, and the novelty of the term as a
source of humor can all be important factors in determining
the particular choice of animal referenced. It might be
surmised, though, that the preceding three terms common
to baseball folk speech reflect the strong rural influence in
baseball. In the case of the term "chickenshit" it is possible
that the choice of the animal is not so obscure. Commonly, a

person who does not possess a large degree of fortitude or "guts" is said to be "chicken" (i.e., afraid). Similarly, a player who performs an unfair act is considered "chicken" in that he had to resort to iniquitous actions in order to accomplish that which could have been done in a skillful manner. A baseball player watching a Western on television, upon seeing one dueler shoot another in the back, would surely describe the act as "chickenshit".

In discussing the terms "horseshit" or "chickenshit" it is only appropriate to mention the common baseball term "bush", which can be used as a synonym for either of the two. "Bush", which probably originated as a condescending reference by the established players in the Major Leagues to the unkempt and overgrown nature of the playing fields of lesser leagues than the Major Leagues (the so-called "Bush Leagues"), has been extended to denote any action considered not up to standard. That is, it can mean either "low class", as in propping up the rim of one's hat (a transgression of baseball etiquette), or "unnecessary", as in starting a fight with a player on the opposing team who has done nothing to prompt a fight.

Chapter 7

THE FOUR BASIC GROUPS: PRELIMINARIES

The emphasis on the representative roles and status positions of the players results in the analysis of insults according to specific situations as they occur in games. It is important to understand, however, that the complex tension that exists between the individual player as a role type and the individual player as personality can evoke verbal expressions that emphasize personal traits rather than specific actions of the game. That is, insults do not arise exclusively from the functional interactions of the members of the four basic groups acting within the structure of the game. The tension between players' personalities surfaces most obviously in the derogatory comments concerning personal appearance and age, both of which are, in general, primary concerns of Americans. As usual, umpires are also subject to this particular type of abuse.

Not surprisingly, someone who is overweight is most likely to be chided. This might be a reflection of the general dislike that Americans have for overweight people. A large umpire may hear "Hey, ump. Move to the right. You're blocking the infield!" "Blocking" means blocking the view of those watching the game from the dugout. A fat player may be the target of the comment "Let's tap that guy's stomach and have a party!" where his stomach is seen as resembling a keg of beer. To "tap" a keg is to open it. More commonly heard is "One man per uniform!" (or "One man to a pair of pants!"), "You can't let two men bat at once!", or "No fair playing two third basemen!" Also common is "Sit down before someone harpoons you!" The implication here is that the person is so overweight that he resembles a whale. Because this comment does not refer to any aspect of the game itself, it is useful when insulting someone who is not a player - an obnoxious, portly fan, perhaps. Weight problems are also addressed in less direct fashion; sometimes eating habits are alluded to, as in "Take the ball away from him. He looks hungry." which is said to an overweight fielder. Similarly, "Have another doughnut!" sarcastically implies that an overweight player has already had too many and should possibly "Mix in (i.e., have) a salad occasionally". Because personal appearance is not directly related to aspects of the game, taunts of this nature are not usually saved for specific situations. One taunt that is used more specifically, however, is the comment regarding weight that is invoked in the specific circumstance of an overweight defensive player not being able to reach a batted ball that is hit in his vicinity: "You would have had that ball 30 pounds ago!" This implies that his weight has effected his "range" - how far he is able to move to get to a ball. The term "ago" lends the further implication that the player is getting old and is no longer capable of playing his position effectively.

A thin player may also expect not to go unnoticed. He may hear "Where's the rest of the chicken?" which refers to a thin or "chicken" neck. Or, if he is both thin and tall, he may hear "Who suited up the telephone pole?" A short player is usually the recipient of one of the two comments "Get out of the hole!", which attributes his lack of height to his standing in a hole, or "Get off your knees!". A player with large ears may be called a "cab with both doors open". An older player may be the target of the question "Isn't there an age limit in this league?!" or sometimes, simply, "Get older."

Chapter 8
THE UMPIRES

Of the four basic groups, only the umpires are not strictly "playing" the game. Their purpose is to pass judgement on the events that occur during the game. Among all of the four basic groups, they are outsiders; within the structure of the game they have no "home". In fact, one of the worst things that an umpire can be called is a "homer", someone who is favoring — protecting — the home team. Though the term is used much more often in an attempt to pressure the umpire than as an expression of fact, there are times when umpires do, in fact, give the home team the benefit of the doubt on a large percentage of the close calls. This is not the case in professional baseball where the umpires are professional, but mostly in games involving teams in remote areas or in extremely partisan towns where the umpire is a local resident and possibly friendly with some of the players on the team. There are even more extreme cases. Some semi-professional teams play prison teams in their locality. In these games often the umpires are themselves convicts. Such umpires may have more at stake than just verbal abuse if they upset their fellow convicts on the prison team with a bad call. As a result, many calls in these games are ruled in favor of the home team.

The relationship between players and umpires is often
an antagonistic one and thus the source of much taunting.
Because of the pressure on players to perform well, the
umpires (or "Blue", as they are often referred to, in reference
to their uniform color) are often the target of the players'
frustrations. Their anxiety can be intensified by the fact
that the players are out in the open where everyone may
observe their mistakes. This serves to heighten their sense
of embarrassment. It is often the umpire, the one who has
passed judgement, who takes the brunt of the players'
emotional outbursts. The umpires represent an objective
opinion, being a member of neither team. But it is this
detachment that is the source of much of the tension
between the players and the umpires. Since the umpire has
the jurisdiction to rule on what is a mistake or a failure, he
enters the realm of an opposing group. This causes an
emotional tension between players and umpires not only
from the stress inherent in the agonistic structure of
competition, but also from an underlying question of who
defines mistake and failure, on which Everett Hughes
comments (Hughes 1958:93) "a colleague group (the people
who consider themselves subject to the same risks) will
stubbornly defend its own right to define mistakes, and to
say in the given case whether one has been made". To be
sure, the structure of the game also puts the umpires at a
disadvantage. They are employed to officiate a game that
contains a plethora of rules and myriad situations in which
these rules apply. Moreover, the speed of the ball and the
large distances covered in the game result in many
equivocal judgements which can lead to further resentment
against those passing judgement (Redl 1971:417). However,
since umpires have the authority to eject a player from the
game, insults directed at them are often veiled in a cloak of
metaphor and euphemism in order to be less direct, less of a
spectacle of anarchy. Ultimately, the umpires must present
themselves as figures of power and confidence. In turn, the
players try to undermine this image with taunts that

suggest the umpires' sexual inferiority, their impartiality, their laziness, and their general ineptitude.

An umpire must establish himself as a stern, confident figure if he is to be respected and his judgements are to be accepted. Consequently, an umpire cannot allow unlimited verbal abuse from the players. Such treatment could only serve to undermine the respect that he must have in order to keep control of the game. Thus the indirectness of many of the taunts directed to umpires by players also serves as a vehicle to convey the players' anger without presenting an open spectacle of the umpire's presumed incompetence. It is for this reason that a catcher is usually allowed to argue with an umpire as long as he keeps facing the pitcher. Since he is wearing a mask and facing in the other direction, it does not appear that he is arguing, so his show of disrespect for the umpire's judgement is apparent only to the umpire (and the batter, who would most likely be opposing the catcher's viewpoint, anyway, and agreeing with the umpire.) If, however, the catcher turns around to argue, he will quickly be silenced.

A fairly subtle point arises here. If, as I have been contending, the folk speech during games is a shared knowledge of the community, shared even by the umpires, who know the language by continued exposure to it, then it must be true that, to some extent at least, the umpires know what is being said to them, no matter how "indirect" (i.e., couched in metaphor) it is. Moreover, they must also realize that certainly many, if not all, of the players who heard a particular taunt directed at them know what the taunt meant. Is not the effect of a particular insult peculiar to the baseball community then the same as the effect of any other insult in general? That is, is there really any difference between a player telling an umpire that "You have your head up your ass!" or, equivalently, "You have a glass stomach!" (through which his head, which is up his ass, can see), since, in sharing the knowledge of the meaning of the last insult with the other members of the baseball community, the umpire understands the equivalence of the two insults? Certainly there is a difference. For in adopting both the structure and content of language common to the particular culture (the baseball community) the vocal agressor (the player) acts within the framework of accepted rules of that culture. He is, in a sense, acting within a role type, rather than a personality, that functions in the structure of accepted standards of personal interaction in the game. A general insult (i.e., one that is not peculiar to the baseball community), in existing outside of the sphere of language employed exclusively by the baseball community, signals a removal of the speaker from his role type, placing him as an individual personality pitted against another personality, the umpire. In this perspective, an insult is a personal affront to an individual and is considered offensive. The extent to which an umpire accepts the abuse directed towards him in some sense defines the limits to which he is able to act out his role as the silent, unaffected, objective judge. Clearly, the boundary of these limits is defined at the border between the umpire as role type and the umpire as personality, where pride and self-esteem may override role type influences.

Not surprisingly, the umpires' eyesight is a common target of the players' taunts. It is common to imply that an umpire has very poor eyesight, or is even blind, and hence is insufficient for his job. For instance, if an umpire calls an apparent "strike" a "ball", the defensive team may yell "sounds low", implying that the umpire cannot see the ball and is merely listening for it. In general, if a player does not agree with an umpire's call, he may yell "Kick his dog. He'll wake up." where "he" refers to the umpire. The reference here is to seeing-eye dogs, which are used to aid blind people, thus attributing the umpire's poor judgement to blindness. Furthermore, it suggests that the umpire is so inept that not only is he physically unable to perform well, but that he lacks the proper motivation for the job, as he has fallen asleep in the middle of the game. Variations of this comment are "Kick your dog!" and "Ask your dog!" in which the umpire's judgement is no better than his dog's. These taunts are indirect enough that they do not usually prompt a player's ejection, even though the umpire's mental and physical condition have been brought into question. Often the most imaginative taunts are saved for the most tense and emotional situations so that the sympathetic reaction of the audience to the speaker's comments is enhanced, increasing the audience's anti-pathetic response to the umpire's actions. If an umpire "misses" a call (makes poor judgement) in a critical situation, he may hear "If you had one more eye you'd be a Cyclops!" which implies that at the moment, the umpire is without eyes, making him somewhat ill-equipped for his job. The suggestion of an umpire's blindness may also be an attempt to portray him as sexually inferior, as blindness can be symbolic of emasculation (Dundes 1980:113).

Not all of the umpires' visual problems are attributed to blindness. Some insults simply suggest that the umpire's judgement is being adversely affected by the elements around him, such as the field and his own equipment. These comments suggest that the umpire is being overwhelmed by his surroundings, which is a further portrayal of the umpire as an outsider. A disagreeable call may prompt "Dust off the plate!", a demand to clean the dirt, which is presumably obstructing the umpire's vision, off of the plate. A general series of bad calls will prompt "Look through the bars, not at them!". The "bars" are the protective bars across the home plate umpire's mask. In a similar sense is "Punch a hole in that mask!" — a hole to see through, that is. A more specific case is that of the home plate umpire making a series of similar close calls consecutively — calling several consecutive balls, which upsets the defensive team, or several consecutive strikes, which upsets the offensive team. In this situation, it is common to hear the offended

team yell, "Shake your head. Your eyes are stuck!",
meaning that the umpire can see only one part of the plate
and is making the calls as if the ball went where he was
looking, whether it did or not. This portrays the umpire in a
humorously rigid position; a rigidity equated with his job as
an enforcer of the rules. If an umpire calls a "ball" on a pitch
that is very close to the inside or outside edge (the "corners")
of the plate the defensive team will often yell "The plate has
corners!", implying that the umpire could not see the
corners of the plate during the pitch. An umpire unable to
see the entire plate would undoubtably have problems in
"calling" pitches. A pitch that appears to be right over the
middle of the plate but is not called a strike will often
prompt the exhortation "That cut the plate in half!" from
the opposition, who feel that a strike should have been
called. The common phrase "Get your head out of your ass!"
is often directed towards umpires. This implies that the
umpire is not able to see very well, being in such a
precarious and possibly sexually submissive position
(bending over).

It is not uncommon for the umpire's motivation to be
questioned. The usual implication is that he is either lazy or
favoring the other team. A team that is upset with an
umpire's performance may make the suggestion to "Pull up
a chair, ump. You're missing a good game!", the connotation being that the umpire is not paying attention to the
game, as he is "missing" it — not seeing it. Since to "miss" a
call means to judge it incorrectly, "missing" further
implicates the umpire's judgement. The umpire is also
being depicted as lazy and not really involved in the game
to the extent he should be. Thus he should "pull up a chair"
like the rest of the crowd, who are also not participating in
the game. In the late inning of a game, an umpire that
appears to be making decisions hastily may be asked,
"Steak on the table?" implying that he is in a rush to get
home for dinner and is making calls — right or wrong —

that will speed up the game. This is consistent with the notion that, within the structure of the game itself, the umpire is without a home. Whereas the players strive to get to "home" base on the field during the game, the umpire must quit the game and leave the field in order to get home. This is another comment that contains the hint of the tension which exists between the group of baseball players and the group of umpires as a result of the structure of the game. In the opposite case in which an umpire is not calling enough strikes to please the defensive team, that team may ask, "Is your right arm tied down?", the right arm being the one used by the home plate umpire to signal for a strike (and all of the umpires to signal for an out).

It is also common for players to suggest that an umpire is being partial to one team. This is another attempt that the players make at attacking the basic requirements of a good umpire; in this case, impartiality. If a player suggests that there are "Ten men on the field!", he is implying that, in addition to the usual nine defensive players on the field, the umpire is, in effect, also acting as a member of the defensive team, since he is helping them so much. The question of impartiality is also addressed when a player yells, "Call 'em both ways!" which implies that the umpire is not "calling" — umpiring — the game similarly for both teams. Finally, it is sometimes suggested that the umpire's decisions are made purely as a matter of chance. In this vein is "Flip a coin!", where the umpire's decision is based on the toss of a coin. Similar implications exist in "Wait for the coin to drop!", in which the umpire is seen as too impatient to follow his own system of chance and thus his decision becomes totally arbitrary. This haphazard approach to umpiring is also suggested in the term "neighborhood call" — a pitch that was called a strike because it was merely in the neighborhood of (i.e., near) the plate. In general, players who are disgusted with an umpire's overall performance may resort to grand generalities that suggest that the umpire is ruining the entire game. Examples of this are "You're killing us, ump!" and "You're taking us out of the ball game!"

It should be noted that the home plate umpire is the primary target of derision among the umpires as it is he who makes the majority of calls during the course of a game. It is the great variety of situations upon which he rules that results in the generation of the many situation-dependent taunts directed toward him. Take, for example, a situation in which the "count" on a particular batter is three balls and no strikes. It is often a good idea to "take" (make no attempt at) the next pitch thrown since if it is a ball, the batter is entitled to first base ("walked"), and if it is a strike the batter still has a significant advantage over the pitcher. A pitcher will often anticipate this situation and attempt to enhance his odds of throwing a strike by trying to throw the pitch over the middle of the plate. Now, if the pitch is near the edge of the strike zone and called a "strike" by the umpire, it is often assumed by the offensive team that the call was influenced by the umpire's anticipation of the pitcher throwing a strike because of the circumstances. Thus the frequently heard comment from the offensive team in this situation is "It's not automatic, ump!" This is said almost exclusively in the situation when the "count" on the batter is at three balls and no strikes. Comments such as this one are good indicators of the degree to which baseball players are concerned with what the opponent is thinking during a game. One reason that this exoteric dimension arises is that baseball is a stategic game on many levels and it can be advantageous for a team to consider what the other team is thinking and what their possible strategy might be.

Another specific situation that elicits a specific comment is the attempt by a batter who has been "fooled" by a pitch to stop his swing; first thinking it was a strike, then trying to hold back or "check" his swing when he realizes that the pitch is not going to be in the strike zone. If the umpire decides that the pitch was indeed a "ball" he must then also decide whether or not the player stopped his swing in time. (If he did not, it is a "strike".) If the umpire judges that he did indeed stop his swing in time and calls the pitch a "ball", a player (or often the manager) on the opposition will often yell, "If he'd 'ave hit it, it would have gone out of the ball park!", implying both that the batter took a full swing and that the pitch should have been called a "strike".

Chapter 9
THE FIELDERS

The fielders perform only defensive functions. They are, in a sense, always in a submissive position in which they have to receive the attacks of the opposition unless they can defend themselves by relying on their agility and dexterity. Consequently, the taunts directed towards fielders often portray them as being clumsy and imply a sexual inferiority in those who cannot control their bodies. Not surprisingly, a common reference is to a defensive player's hands. A player who handles hard hit balls well is said to have "soft" hands and can really "pick it", as opposed to someone who has "bad" or "hubcap" hands (since the ball bounces off of them as if they were metal). It may be suggested that such a fielder should go to the junkyard to get a new mitt. Such a player is sometimes said to "butcher" or "beat the hell out of" the ball.

Many of the taunts to fielders concern the notion of control, as in "Find the handle!", where a "handle" is just a reference to something that is grabbed to gain control. This is said to a player who drops or juggles the ball. Food is also a common element of these taunts. This may stem from the fact that people often eat while watching baseball games and thus food is often associated with the ball park. It may also be a by-product of the home base being called "the plate", "the dish" or, a now obsolete term, "the pan". It is interesting to try and reconcile the two seemingly unrelated subjects of food and fielding by approaching fielding — the capture, control, and manipulation of the ball on defense — from a psychoanalytic perspective. The study of ball games among children has interested psychoanalysts as a method of learning more about the psychological development of children who are attempting to gain control, both physical and mental, of the sexual funtioning of their bodies. Psychoanalysts such as Melanie Klein noted long ago the association of ball games with sexual activity in which "Speech and pleasure in motion have always a libidinal cathexis of a genital-symbolic nature" (Klein 1926:61). This cathexis involves the identification of hands, feet, etc., with the penis, the control of which represents sexual control (Stokes 1956:185-192). Further, an early association of "impregnation through eating" (Klein 1926:53) results in a "tendency to make ritual and verbal associations between eating and sexual intercourse" (Leach 1964:42). The application of these theories can shed some light on the sometimes abstruse taunts yelled at the fielders.

All of these factors may be influential in the reference to food in taunts concerning fielding which imply sexual incompetence or inferiority. For instance, if a player manages to knock the ball down but has trouble getting control of it, he may be told to "Stick a fork in it!", where the ball is controlled by penetration with a fork. The inability of the player to control the ball is transferred to an inability to penetrate the object to be controlled, thus suggesting sexual incompetence. The fact that a fork is the penetrating tool implies that the object to be penetrated is an edible substance, again exhibiting the relationship between food and sexual activity. Another taunt that is heard in this situation is "Follow it around and see what it eats!". Here the ball is seen as living and with conscious intentions of avoiding the defensive player. This expression is possibly influenced by Leach's theory of the link of food to sexual activity by (Leach 1964:23-63) "correspondence between categories of sexual accessibility and the categories of (animal) edibility". Interestingly, a ground ball that a fielder cannot handle is said to "eat him up". This might suggest that the edibility of the fielder represents his vulnerability to attack. This general notion of the existence of a symbolic relationship between edibility and vulnerability is well supported by taunts directed at the pitcher, which will be discussed later. It is interesting to note that a common term for misplaying a ball is to "boot" the ball, which is also a common slang term for "throwing up". Hence there may be a connection here between not being able to handle a ball and not being able to eat or handle food correctly, both possibly expressing a lack of sexual competence. These ideas are convolved in the statement made to a fielder that has just fumbled a ball: "Do you eat with those hands?!" The implication is that the player's hands are useless for performing even such simple tasks as handling food and that his lack of bodily control represents a lack of control over his sexual functions.

There are some comments, of course, that do not reflect sexual undercurrents. If a ball is hit very hard past an infielder, an opposing player might tell him to "Get the license number!". The defensive player has been the victim of a sort of hit and run and can only identify the perpetrator as it escapes him. If the ball hits the defensive player's foot as he stoops to field it, he will most likely hear "Put a glove on that foot!". In general, a poor defensive player may be asked, "Is that glove an ornament?" suggesting that it serves purely decorative purposes since the player evidently does not know how to use it.

Two other aspects of the game that influence the use of slang by, and directed to, infielders are directly related to the concept of spatial enhancement. The fact that the fielders are spread out over a significantly large area is a deterrent to the use of slang by the fielders themselves. This is simply because it is somewhat difficult to keep up lively conversation at large distances. Secondly, the concept of a "team" may also be somewhat diminished by the spatial separation of the players. Players stand out more as individuals when standing in the wide open spaces of the baseball field. This is exactly what the opposition preys on when yelling at fielders. An error by a fielder happens out in the open, which serves to emphasize the singularity of fault and can increase the anxiety felt by the erring fielder.

There are taunts that focus on the general actions common to all fielders such as fielding and throwing and are thus less situational. Any ball that is thrown over an intended player's head may prompt the opposition to yell, "Do you serve drinks on that flight?!". Or, if a ball is thrown with a high arc, "Drawing rain out there!". In general, if a poor throw is made, some comment is made about the player's throwing abilities or, possibly, about the condition of his arm, such as "If your arm hurts, go to the hospital!" which implies both that the player's arm is ineffective and that he should not be in the game. It is also reflective of the general fear that players have of injuring their arms, a fairly common and always feared occurrence.

Certain very specific situations elicit specific taunts. One particular case is the attempt by a catcher to throw out a player who is trying to "steal" a base (attempting to gain possession of a base without the help of a hit, error, or walk). The situation usually involves the "stealing" of second base. If the catcher throws the ball in the dirt in front of second base, he is likely to hear, "Cut second!" from the opposition. To "cut" a ball is to relay it from one player to another (on the demand "cut!") on a play that requires the ball to be transferred a long distance. The implication here, then, is that the distance between home plate and second base is too far for the catcher to throw because of his poor throwing ability. Of course, any catcher can throw the ball that distance, so the preposterousness of what the taunt implies enhances the force of the insult. The command "cut" is normally used by the defense for strategic purposes and thus its use by the offense is, in itself, somewhat of an insult to the defense. The insulted group's own language is being used to taunt them. In general, the act of employing an item of folk speech of another group for the purpose of taunting that group can be a particularly effective method of insulting. In mocking the use of the item, one mocks the actions, and the values implicitly related to those actions, that give rise to that item.

One might sense that we are approaching an apparent inconsistency, or at least an ambiguity, in this line of argument since we are discussing a taunt from one baseball player to another. In mocking the actions (hence, values) of another baseball player is he not inherently mocking his own? He is not. And it is the existence of folk subgroups that is exactly the reason why he is not, and why there is no inconsistency in the above argument. Notice that the taunting is directed not at every member of the other team but to a specific group on the other team - the fielders. It is necessary to differentiate the fielders from their teammates in keeping with the concept of a target auditor. The fielders are a folk subgroup since they exist as members of the folk group of baseball players yet can be distinguished from other players during the game. That is, their function - fielding - further defines them as a group. Since they can be considered a separate (sub)group, then one would expect them to possess a specialized language. In fact, they do. There are many concise expressions used by fielders for the purpose of quick, accurate communication, which is essential for performing as an effective defensive unit. An example is the aforementioned "cut".[1] Communication between fielders is essential to a strong defense for many strategic reasons, including the positioning of players, so a poorly positioned outfielder might be told to "Get in the zip code!", suggesting that he might be positioned a bit far from home plate.

Yet one may wish to pursue this issue further and ask that, since all fielders are also hitters, and vice versa, during the course of a game, is it really possible to consider them each as separate subgoups, since it is just the same people performing different functions? The answer is yes and it illustrates a concept of central importance; namely, how the function of folk speech is inextricably tied to the performance. Since the performance depends upon the situation in which the performer exists at the time, the context of the situation must be considered. And, since the context within which a performer acts can be related to the function that he performs within a group (such as players in the game) the function an item of folk speech performs can be related to the function that the speaker performs as a member of his group. Hence, even though the players that are on defense are the same players that will be on offense, their status as members of a particular folk (sub)group changes! They are members of one subgroup when on offense, and another when on defense. In changing their function, they change their relationship to both the other players in the game as well as to the structure of the game. Yet all the time they remain within the group of baseball players. This concept of the "folk subgroup" is very important to consider. It is not enough to consider an individual as solely the member of one fixed folk group and it is still not enough to categorize an individual as a member of a number of static folk groups or subgroups, although in some cases that is the situation. The generalization that must be made is that individuals can be members of more than one folk group as well as a member of one or more subgroups within these groups, and that they may shift in an out of these groups and subgroups. Thus it is necessary to consider how the interpretive community in which a performer or an auditor resides changes their perception of their roles.

Chapter 10
THE HITTERS

The struggle for power between the hitter and the pitcher is a constant source of tension in which, very often, the intense dramatic conflict on the field evokes expressions of the unconscious struggle for sexual dominance that can arise between male combatants, surfacing through formal verbal devices. This is due, in part, to the fact that the possiblity exists that either the pitcher or the batter may achieve complete success against one another. A pitcher can retire the batter by getting him "out". The batter, being defeated, is dismissed from an active role in the offensive activities of his team until his next turn at bat. However, if the batter gets a "hit", he is able to occupy a base and the pitcher must try his luck with the next batter. These clearly delineated victories and defeats are unequivocal triumphs of one participant over the other and the possibility of their occurrence sets the batter and the pitcher in an intense emotional opposition to each other.

Intensifying this conflict is the possibility that these complete victories may be even more glorious and take on the dimension of perfection for which each pitcher or hitter strives. The pitcher may "strike out" the batter (register three strikes against him) in which case the batter must immediately return to the dugout; he is not even able to enjoy the brief moments of excitement which may accompany other types of "outs". Unlike a batter who is retired by a "ground out" or a "fly out", he does not experience hitting the ball, that simultaneous assault on the senses in which the force of the ball hitting the bat and the sound of such contact combine to give the batter an instant, if short lived, euphoria. The unmistakable sensations of the jolt in his arms and the crack of sound in his ears is replaced by the silence of defeat. Nor does he get to run hastily to first base in an attempt to "beat out" (arrive before the throw) a "ground ball", or maybe see a long fly rise into the blue sky before settling into the glove of an outfielder. He must simply return to the dugout — a slow march of defeat in front of his teammates, the opposition, and the spectators.

On the other hand, the batter is able to achieve a complete and perfect success against the pitcher by hitting a "home run". A ball hit over the fence allows all runners on the bases, as well as the batter himself, to score. Not only do they score, but they do it at their own pace. The passage of the ball over the fence, according to the rules, allows all runners and the batter to score automatically, so it is not necessary for them to run. The result is a triumphant jaunt around the bases by the batter at his own desired pace. Since it is often important for the pitcher to set the pace of a game to conform to his pitching style, such a show is not only upsetting to the pitcher because it represents his defeat in a battle of skill, but also because it disrupts the pace of the game. For the batter, it is not only a show of victory but a show of control. He shows that he can control the pace of the game. And the pitcher can only watch as he slowly circles the bases and receives the triumphant greetings of his teammates at "home plate".

Complete dominance in the dramatic action of the game can be manifest in the symbolic representation of sexual dominance by either the pitcher or the hitter.

Teammates try to bolster the hitter's confidence with comments that suggest the hitter's sexual domination of the pitcher, such as "Jump on him (the pitcher)!" or "Jump all over him!", meaning to be aggressive and alert and "attack" the ball. The attainment of a hit is seen as a personal attack on the pitcher. These comments are also a metaphorical sexual threat to the pitcher since to "jump on" someone, in the folk speech of many American youths, is to initiate some form of sexual activity. The embarrassment and humiliation that the batter wishes to inflict upon the pitcher by hitting the ball, by dominating him, is in some sense connotative of sexual domination, not an uncommon theme in all-male sports (Dundes 1980:199-210). Interestingly, a good hitter is often called a "stud". Though there is no implied reference to sexual abilities by the speaker, it is interesting to note the use of a term relating a person possessing sexual expertise to a hitter who is adept with, and in control of, the bat. The equation of sexual control and the control that a hitter possesses is evident in the description of a pitch in the most desirable spot of the strike zone (at about the height of the waist) as "cock high". The ball, in being at about the same place as the "cock" (penis), is said to be easy to "handle" (synonymous with "attack"). This asserts the hitter's literal control of the bat and subconsciously reaffirms control of his sexual apparatus and his sexual (physical) superiority to the pitcher.

At any time during an "at-bat", a hitter may hear his teammates instruct him to "Take him (the pitcher) deep!", "Take him over the wall!" , or "Lose him!"; that is, hit a home run. The first comment derives from the fact that a home run is invariably a ball that has been hit "deep" (far) into the outfield. Further, "deep" suggests a sexual penetration — physical domination — of the pitcher by the batter. Often the ball is hit over a fence and thus "lost", whence the second remark. Alternatively, a home run may have the effect of "losing" the pitcher as his coach may take him out of the game as a result. Because of the metonymous nature of these comments, they become a more personal attack on the pitcher as it is he, rather than the ball, that is being "lost" or "taken deep".[1] In representing the ball as an extension of the pitcher (take 'him' over the wall), there is often a symbolic displacement of sexual domination from the pitcher to the ball. For instance, to hit a ball hard is to "pop" the ball. While there is quite possibly an onomato-poeic significance to the term, it also strongly suggests defloration. A stronger homosexual component is evident in the description of someone who "hit the shit out of the ball" (hit it very hard). If the ball contains feces, it becomes analogous to the anus. Thus an attack upon it is symbolic of the hitter's phallic thrusts at his opponent and the expulsion of the feces signals penetration of the phallus and attainment of sexual domination. These expressions give strong evidence against Stokes' contention that (Stokes 1956:187) "the ball is itself the phallus."

In the more specific instance of the pitcher having two strikes on the hitter, a hitter's teammates will often say, "Get a piece!". That is, make contact with a "piece" of the ball and "stay alive" by "hanging tough" and not striking out. The reference to life and death as a metaphorical representation of a hitter's success or failure is also evident in the comment which is reserved for the specific situation in which a defensive player drops a foul fly ball. The exhortation from the hitter's dugout is invariably "New life!". This stems from the fact that the hitter was, in a sense, brought back from the dead as a foul ball fly ball, if playable, is usually an "easy out". Thus the hitter was in great danger of being "eliminated". His escape was (presumably) like returning from the dead, both unexpected and a great relief. The reference to life and death is also evident in the description of a player who has been thrown out on the bases. He is said to have been "gunned down" or "wiped out". Similarly, a double play is called a "twin killing" and runners left on base at the end of an inning are said to have "died on base".

In general, players are taunted when they are still at the plate (as opposed to walking away — after an out, for instance) since the primary objective of those doing the taunting is to hinder a player's performance of an action. Usually, the worse a player is performing, the more he will be taunted. It is usually not hard to tell when a player is floundering at the plate. If such a player has "taken" a pitch (let it go by without attempting to swing at it) because he was obviously badly fooled, thinking it would be a "ball", he may be told by the opposition to "Take two and go to right!". This is not really a sarcastic suggestion but a statement of the assumed course of events. Here a poor hitter is characterized as someone who "takes" two strikes (the implication being that he was fooled by them) and then, in an act of desperation, lunges at the ball and hits it weakly. "Right" refers to right field, where a weak right handed hitter would most likely place a poorly hit ball. This comment seems to have developed with a preference for right-handed batters, probably because of their abundance. Though it could easily be adapted to apply to left-handed hitters ("Take two and go to left!"), it is not done.

Even if the batter manages to hit the ball, there are suggestions that he did not do it well. If the ball is not hit with much force, it may be a "dribbler", if it is hit on the ground, or a "bleeder", if it is hit in the air just out of reach of the fielders. Either of these may have been a "tweener" if it was hit just between two players. It might be said of a "dribbler" that was a "tweener" that "The ball had eyes!", an imaginative explanation for the reason that the ball was able to find its way between the fielders. "Tweener" is also used to describe a ball hit very hard between the outfielders — in the "alley", that is. The term "bleeder" may have originated from considerations similar to those resulting in the term "wounded duck" for a poorly thrown football, where slow or awkward flight is compared to the movements of a wounded and bleeding bird. There are some interesting second order taunts derived from the primary term "bleeder". When an opposing player hits a "bleeder" he is likely to hear "Wipe the blood off the bat!", "Wipe the blood off the ball", or "Put a Band-Aid on that thing!", where "thing" refers to either the ball or the bat.

On the other hand, for the batter who does get a good hit, there are an array of expressions used by his teammtes to highlight that fact. These comments not only serve to express the joy of achievement but also to prolong the agony of the opponent, who must not only suffer the physical defeat, but must also listen to the derogatory comments from the opposition. One common method of expression is the use of sarcasm to suggest that a particular act was the performed to perfection. Although the use of sarcasm is often used as a means of derision (as in the aforementioned "Nice mind!"), to imply the nonexistence or poor quality of an object, teammates use it to suggest that something has reached its peak. For instance, if a batter hits a ball extremely hard, a "wicked shot" perhaps, his teammates may say to him "Hit it harder!", implying that the ball could not have been hit any harder.

The ultimate achievement for the hitter in his battle against the pitcher is the hitting of a home run. Hence teammates of the hitter find the occasion of a home run a perfect time to chastise the pitcher. In the event of a home run, as the batter is circling the bases, the pitcher may have no choice but to listen to a teammate of the hitter yell, "Dial long distance. And charge it to the pitcher!". The analogy of the long distance hit and the long distance phone call also gives rise to the description of someone who hit a home run as someone who "dialed 8", since the phones in the hotels that the players stay in when traveling usually require that an "8" be dialed before a long distance phone call be made.

These expressions further illustrate the influx of elements of everyday life into the folk speech of baseball players. In fact, to hit a home run is to "hit it downtown", because in some of the ballparks, such as Wrigley Field in Chicago, a ball hit over the outfield fence will very often land on the city streets outside of the stadium. Imaginative use of common objects, places, or actions enhances the reality of the outside world within the world of play, reaffirming the social nature of the baseball community. It is also a colorful method of description. A batter is not "given permission" to swing at a pitch in the situation when the count is three balls and no strikes (a situation in which it is usually to a hitter's advantage to let the pitch go by — "take" the pitch — in order to pressure the pitcher to throw a strike); he is "given the green light".

The symbolic sexual transference to the ball is also evident in the expression "get a piece" since, in its use among American youths, it is an abbreviated form of "get a piece of ass", a common expression referring to hetero-sexual sexual intercourse.[2] The connection being made between the two uses of this particular expression is not random. As an example of just how close a connection there may be in the mind of the performers (or audience) between the literal meaning of an expression and the underlying symbolism, I will relate an incident that occured during a game. It was a particularly tense situation in an important game and there was a good deal of taunting going on by members of both teams. The batter on team A had two strikes on him. The next pitch was a curve ball on the outside corner of the plate that fooled him badly. He was only able to make an awkward swing at the ball, barely making contact with the ball, which he "fouled off" behind him. A player on the opposition, team B, yelled at the hitter from the dugout, "You were lucky to get a piece!", implying that he was lucky to have even touched the ball, having been fooled so badly. A teammate of the batter, attempting to negate the sympathetic response that the player on team B had evoked from the audience at the expense of the hitter, retorted, "So was your mother!". The implication that the player's mother was "lucky to get a piece" refers not to the literal use of the term as it applied to baseball, but to the sexually symbolic meaning. In this context, the meaning of "get a piece" no longer referred to hitting the ball but to sexual intercourse. The suggestion that the mother of the player on team B was lucky to find anyone with whom to have sexual intercourse implies not only that she is very unattractive but, because of general notion of her looking for someone for such an activity, suggests a range of less than flattering possibilities. One possibility is that she was looking for a husband, an attempt that may have been unsuccessful, thus implying that the outspoken player on team B who was taunting the batter is a bastard. In any case, to comment on the sexual activity of a person's mother is offensive in itself. This type of insult is not so common in baseball taunts, as it falls outside of the realm of subjects relating to the game itself. It is more consistent with the more personal insults used, for instance, in black street culture[3] or, to a lesser extent, among American youths. The importance of this comment to our discussion, however, is to underscore the relationship between the literal meaning of taunts and the underlying symbolism, which may or may not exist in the conscious mind of the performer.

Some of the supportive comments that are said before a hitter comes to the plate reflect the position of the hitter as an attacker of the defensive team's home. The hitter is urged to lead an assault and "Get a foot in the door." and start a "rally" (a barrage of hits and runs) or take control and "Get in the driver's seat." His attack on the pitcher becomes an attack on the pitcher's possessions — his home and his car. If a team is not doing well, a batter's teammate might tell him to "Be a pioneer!" and be the first to enter the opposition's territory. This comment resonates with the rural element in baseball and underscores the struggle between the teams to gain possession of the territory, the region of land called the "field". The players work in conjunction with, and in a sense tame, the wilderness, the field. This can be seen in the players' terms for the playing area. The "field" is often called the "park", suggesting not a wilderness area such as a field, but a region that has become a friendly place — a park. In turn, the playing area can even come to represent an element of the home: teammates may instruct a hitter to "Take him out of the yard!" (i.e., "hit a home run"), which might be made easier if there is a "short porch" (a fence not far from home plate) in the outfield. Both "yards" and "porches" are elements of home life.

In contrast to the supportive nature of teammates' comments, a hitter may expect to receive highly critical taunts from the opposition, who continually try to break his concentration and confidence. Often the batter that is derided the most is one who is not very talented, possibly due to his unaggressive attitude. A batter who appears to be lackadaisical at the plate may be told "Take the bat off your shoulder!" or asked "Is that bat a decoration?!" implying that the bat is being used for purely ornamental purposes. Further, a poor hitter is likely to have a lower degree of concentration (which may be either the cause or the effect of his lack of talent). Consequently, he is more likely to be affected by taunts. A hitter who is fooled by a good curve ball and jumps from the plate [that is, "steps in the bucket", a reference to the water bucket that used to be kept in dugouts (Lee 1926:369-370)] is said to have "bailed out" of the "box" (the area designated for hitting by a rectangular chalk line). From this derives the second order taunt "Open your parachute!" which implies that the batter has abandoned his position just as a pilot bails out of an airplane that is in distress. Even after a hitter strikes out, he is likely to be taunted on his way back to the dugout with comments such as "Take a seat!" or "Go grab some bench!", referring to the wooden bench in the dugout. (Hence a player that is not in the line-up is said to be "riding the pine".) The player who is having a particularly bad day and has no hits may be asked "Is it true you got a hit last year?". If a player who had previously been hitless in a few trips to the plate finally manages to get a hit, it is often simply attributed to the "Law of averages!". This comment is consistent with the attention paid to statistics in baseball. Needless to say, the player who has not gotten any hits is particularly apt to be taunted since his confidence might be somewhat diminished and his poor performance is a natural target for derision. Consequently, there are a particular group of taunts set aside for the player who is having an "Oh-for" day; zero hits in any amount of "at-bats". (It is common to give a players batting record in the form: number of hits per number of times at bat.) It might be suggested (loudly) by the opposition that the player's performance is representative of his talent (or lack thereof) in general and that he is probably "Oh-for-June" or even "Oh-for-career".

Chapter 11
THE PITCHERS

One of the most important players in the game is the pitcher. His influence on the outcome of the game can be greater than any of the other players. He has the ability to single-handedly retire every batter he faces in the game. Yet he is also one of the most vulnerable players in the game, being continually subject to the attacks of the different batters. A good pitching performance may be just about all a team needs to defeat their opponent. But a pitcher who is struggling can become rattled quite quickly if the offensive pressure against him is severe. This can quickly lead to his team's demise. Often the opposition will include a verbal assault along with their physical attack in order to increase the pressure on the pitcher. Since the pitcher is involved in every play that takes place during a game, there are many opportunities for him to make mistakes. Hence he is often being taunted. Because of the many opportunities for his chastisement, the slang directed at him becomes very situational. Since the pitcher is so vital to a team's success, the opposing team is quick to detect any weakening in his performance. The opposition singles out the pitcher as a target for derision even before the game begins. For instance, a player may say that the opposing pitcher "has a fastball and a fastball" which means that his repertoire of pitches consists of one pitch. This would eliminate the element of surprise for the hitters, who would undoubtedly profit from such a situation. Of course, this is not normally the situation. The contest between the pitcher and the hitter is as much a battle of wits as it is a battle of force. However, it is the physical struggle for power between the pitcher and the hitter which provides a basis of conscious tension that gives rise to taunts that try to undermine the pitcher's power by insulting his sexual competence, as well as threatening the defensive area — his home — that he protects. The resulting language is often very aggressive in nature. For instance, teammates may instruct a pitcher to "Smoke him inside!" if they think the pitcher should throw a fastball ("smoke") on the part of the plate closest to the hitter ("inside").

In general, the offensive team taunts the pitcher by suggesting that he is not in control of the game and that he is powerless against their offense. For instance, if the offensive team is getting many hits, they may tell the pitcher "We own you!", implying that they are in complete control and can get hits as often as they please. There is also the implication of sexual dominance implied in the concept of ownership. In the same vein is "We're all over you!". Note that to be "all over" someone is a common expression among American youths meaning to be engaged in some form of sexual activity.

The pitcher is very often taunted about particular aspects of his pitching style, method, or results. If a pitcher throws a "fat" pitch (i.e., one that is easy to hit) he may hear "You want a meathook for that pitch?". The connotation is equivalent to that implied by describing an easily hit pitch as one that is "served on a platter". In a sense, these comments imply that the pitcher is purposely giving the batter an easy pitch to hit. This suggests that he is no longer opposing the hitter but has, possibly, just given up.

Furthermore, the fact that the pitch is on a platter suggests that it is food, ready to be eaten, that is being "served" to the hitter. This is symbolic of the vulnerability of the pitcher to attack, to consumption and destruction; just as a batted ball that the fielder cannot handle is said to "eat him up". The hitter has become the figure of control and is dominating the pitcher who is "serving" him. This may be an allusion to being "serviced" — provided sexual favors — in which case the pitcher has been put in a submissive sexual position relative to the hitter, who is thus seen as a sexually competent, and dominating, person. The association of food and sexual activity that arose in the analysis of the taunts directed at the fielders again gives rise to comments suggestive of Leach's connection between food and sexual activity and suggests the interpretation that food that is to be eaten is symbolic of something prone to sexual attack. An easily hit pitch is "fat" and the common description of an ineffective pitcher is that he is "meat", as in "He's meat." Similarly, a pitch that a batter thought was easy to hit is also described as meat, as in "It was meat." A similar confluence of food and sexual dominance is evident in "Stick a fork in him. He's done." which is said to a pitcher who is doing poorly and is "through" or "done" for the day. The opposition sees him again as a piece of "meat" which is traditionally tested for readiness by poking it with a fork. At the same time, the pitcher is being penetrated. In this light, the speaker's team may be seen as sexually dominant, and the pitcher humiliated by their attacks. A pitcher that is taken out of the game because the offense has gotten many hits off of him is said to have been "Knocked out of the box" or simply "knocked out", as opposed to "going the distance" and finishing the game. Interestingly, these terms are very similar to two boxing terms. Whether or not these terms derived from boxing folk speech, where "knocked out" means to be knocked unconscious and "going the distance" means finishing the fight, is indeterminable, but would not be surprising in light of the intense struggle for power between the pitcher and the hitter.

As the primary defender of the home territory, the pitcher is often subject to taunts that incorporate elements of home life. A team that is threatening to score on the pitcher may yell "We're in your kitchen!". This statement is somewhat abstruse, yet it stresses the fact that the other team is in control of the pitcher's home territory and implies that they have assumed control of the major possessions of the pitcher: his house, his food, and possibly his wife or girl friend (by a traditional, if chauvinistic, connection). However, if a pitcher is doing well in the late innings with his team ahead, his teammates may yell "Close the door!" — finish off the opponent and end the game. This comment may be seen as antithetical to "We're in your kitchen." Here the pitcher is seen as the dominant figure and successfully defending his home. If, however, he is taken out of the game, he is "sent to the showers" (the showers in the locker room). A shower is another item that is commonly thought of in connection with the home.

The pitcher does not need to be "getting hit" for the offensive team to harass him. What prompts the offensive team to even more enthusiastic taunting is a pitcher's "loss of control", his inability to throw strikes. This is most unsettling for a pitcher because it forces him to reconsider his pitching technique. If a pitcher is getting hit hard he can pass is off as a bad day or the luck of the hitters. But if he is unable to throw strikes, it is solely his own fault and he is isolated in his incompetence. Such a situation is ideal for the opposition, who want to increase the pitcher's frustration and embarassment to the point where he is flustered and loses his control even more. A pitcher who has walked a few batters in succession is likely to hear "Squeeze that bar of soap!", suggesting that the ball is as hard to control as a bar of wet soap. Soap is yet another item suggestive of home life.

Sometimes the suggestion is made, sarcastically, that the events are not the pitcher's fault, but due to extraordinary circumstances; he can not throw a strike because the plate is moving — "Tie the plate down!". As usual, the pitcher is being made fun of. This taunt is an example of the way in which the speaker can combine rhetorical strategy and performance to evoke a sympathetic response from the audience (in this case, the speaker's teammates) and create further tension for the target auditor — the struggling pitcher — in an anxiety situation. By projecting the situation into a patently absurd sphere of action, the speaker moves the target auditor away from the situation to the point where he is not actively involved in it. The target auditor is presented with an anxiety situation in which a resolution is being sought but then is moved a mental distance away, farther from an area of control, farther from a solution. Outside of the boundary of the real world frame of reference, the target auditor loses control and his anxiety is increased. In other words, the anxiety produced in the conflict of the real life situation is magnified by projecting the situation into the imaginary frame, outside of the limits of real world solutions. The proposal of preposterous solutions allies the antipathetic force of the insult with the speaker's control to produce a movement away from a potential solution for the target auditor, thus increasing his anxiety.

Continued control problems for the pitcher can make the game proceed very slowly, often making the game somewhat boring even for the team profiting from the pitcher's poor control. Such situations may prompt "You're boring!" or "Get that guy outta there! The fans are leaving!" from the opposition. These comments may reflect the discomfort that baseball players sometimes feel with the image of their game as boring. In general, if things are going badly for a defensive team, the pitcher may be singled out as the target of derision, even though it may not be totally his fault, as in the situation that his team is making a lot of errors "behind him". (In the layout of the field, the fielders are positioned behind the pitcher.) This instance often elicits "Your team hates you!" from the offensive squad. The implication is that the team is purposely making errors because of their dislike for the pitcher. Similarly, if a pitcher is left in the game despite his continuing poor performance, he is told "Your coach hates you!" suggesting that his coach wants him to stay in the game to suffer more abuse. Both these taunts set the pitcher in opposition to not only the opposing team, but to his own teammates as well. The attempt is being made to further alienate the pitcher, who may have to take the blame for all of the defensive malfunctionings of his team, since it is the pitcher, after all, who will get charged with the "loss" in the record books.

A necessary attribute of a good pitcher is that he is tough, both physically and mentally. One aspect of this toughness is the willingness to scare hitters. Fear is important strategically from a pitcher's point of view, since intimidating the hitters can upset their concentration. Since hitting takes the utmost concentration, any deviance from attentiveness brought about by fear will hinder a hitter's performance. To this end, the pitcher may want to throw the ball very close to the batter to "loosen him up" and "keep him honest" (keep him guessing as to what pitch will be thrown next, and where); in short, make him afraid. A pitcher does not want the batter anticipating what pitches will be thrown, and where. A tough pitcher is impartial to who he intimidates he considers every batter his enemy. A tough pitcher is one who would "knock down his grandmother". To "knock down", or "put down", a batter is to make him (or her in this case) "hit the dirt" (that surrounds home plate) in order to avoid a pitch that is thrown at him, usually in the vicinity of the head. That is, he wants to "play some chin music" (throw at his chin) and "spin his cap"; a perfect "purpose pitch" (a pitch that serves the purpose of intimidation) is one that is very close to his head (close enough to touch the bill of his cap) but does not hit him. The phrase "put him down" represents an obvious physical reality yet can also be seen as similar in meaning to its use in verbal dueling where physical domination is often represented in sexual terms; possibly homosexual when used in contests between males. In this case "put him down" could imply "forcing one's adversary to assume a supine position; that is, the 'female position' in typical Western sexual intercourse" (Dundes 1980:203). Thus the pitcher is seen as sexually humiliating the hitter by making him assume the female position in homosexual sexual intercourse. Such imagery also suggests the triumph of the pitcher's will over that of the batter. Since the contest between the pitcher and the hitter is very much a face-to-face confrontation, to be able to turn one contestant away from the battle, physically or mentally, is a victory for the opponent. The ultimate goal of the pitcher is to get the batter out. So, when it comes down to a tight situation, the pitcher will want to throw a strike and will usually offer his best or "out" pitch (since it is most effective in getting people out) and "challenge" the hitter with his best "stuff".

Many insults directed to the pitcher simply comment upon the technical aspects of pitching. If the pitcher is throwing particularly slowly, the opposition may say, "Time him with a sundial! (or "calendar")". To "time" a pitcher is to measure the amount of time it takes for his pitches to reach home plate, thus measuring the velocity of the baseball. To imply that this could be accomplished with a sundial or calendar suggests that the pitcher is not throwing very fast. Another comment often said to a slow pitcher is "Let some air out of that pitch!", as a slow pitch has the appearance of floating like a balloon. This comment is also said to the pitcher when a batter hits the ball a long distance. If a batter hits the ball hard, or when the ball is very poorly thrown (e.g., over the catcher's head or in the dirt) the offense will often yell, "How do ya' hold that pitch?". This is a sarcastic reference to the practice that pitchers have of discussing how one another "holds" — grips — the baseball when throwing a particularly effective pitch. When this comment is directed at the opposition in the above circumstance, it is meant as a joke, since it is unlikely that anyone would want to know how to "hold" a pitch that was particularly ineffective. A common variation of this is "How do you hold your doubles?". Notice again the use of the taunted group's own language by the speaker.If a player hits a ball very hard that is caught for an out, the pitcher may hear "You got 'em popping up!". When a batter hits a fly ball or "pop-up", the pitcher has done his job, since these are easy for the fielders to catch. A hard hit ball low to the ground is not so easy to field. If it is caught, it is a tribute to the fielder's ability, not the pitcher's. The comment is really eluding to the fact that the pitcher has not performed well and was merely lucky that the fielder was able to get the ball.

If the pitcher is "being hit" for a good deal of time, he is likely to hear "How's your neck?". The concern of the offensive team is that the pitcher's neck might be getting sore from turning around quickly to follow the path of yet another hit. This situation may also prompt "Do you want a screen out there?". The "screen" is the protective net that is placed in front of a pitcher who is throwing batting practice. Thus the comment implies both that he needs protection and that he is throwing batting practice (in which the pitcher lets the hitters hit the ball). A pitcher that is prone to the "home run ball" (i.e., he gives up a lot of home runs) may be the target of "Go feed your gopher!". This is a second order term derived from the term "gopher ball" which is synonymous with "home run". This term presumably originated in the early days of baseball when there were no fences (or fences that were far from home plate) and a fielder had to "go for" a ball that was hit past him.

Chapter 12
CONCLUSION

Ultimately the baseball community must be treated as a society in itself, with its own mores and rules. It is often the players' recognition that they exist in a society of their own that promotes both their conduct and their folk speech development. Yet it is also the nature of the game that eventually controls the taunting, as the extensiveness of personal aggressiveness in a contextual performance "must be controlled in some way — by rules and boundaries, or by the distance created between the play world and the real world" (Abrahams 1968:148). Though a good deal of baseball folk speech consists of taunts which serve to create a sense of shame and anger in the opponent, the net overall effect of the use of baseball folk speech among the players is that it unites all the participants in the game as members of the larger group of all baseball players. This acts to not only sustain, but to promote, the development and usage of baseball folk speech.

The latent sexual content of many of the taunts directed toward other players may be a result of cultural factors, impressed on the ballplayers at an early age, surfacing in unconscious channels and circumscribed by formal verbal devices. One such factor might be the atmosphere of competition that often exists between young males trying to prove or express their masculinity. Another important factor might be the repressive nature in which sexual themes are often treated in American society, as well as the repressive mannner in which individuals themselves can be treated by America's economic system. This would be true especially for individuals suffering from economic hardship. Many of the players in this study were of lower income families or were supporting themselves. The repressive elements in American society can affect the individual in a way described by noted psychoanalyst Erik Erikson in his book *Toys and Reasons, Stages in the Ritualization of Experience;* (Erikson 1977:58) "If the human individual, from his ontogenetic beginnings, brings along a substratum that is best circumscribed by the words 'depressive,' 'repressive,' and 'oppressive,' it is once more obvious what the cultural and political setting owes each person in the way of a world view ready to confirm not only the leeway defined by what the senses learn to perceive and the skills to manage, but also a wider vision which will help overcome an always ready sense of vulnerability, impotence, and irreality."

It is particularly interesting to note that the three categories outlined by Erikson as psychological weak points — vulnerability, impotence, and irreality — are those most frequently addressed by baseball players in their folk speech. The feelings of vulnerability are attacked by the individual players' concept of themselves as tough, both physically and mentally, and the feelings of group strength that exist within the context of the team structure. The constant reassertion of sexual prowess and sexual dominance of the opposition is an antidote for the feelings of impotence. And the constant evocation of the mundane materials of life, such as those evident in the formulaic structure "I've seen better A in a B!" and in terms such as "hubcap hands", revitalize the reality of the surrounding world.

The duality of man as role representative and man as personality inherent in both the game of baseball and in modern American society reflects the constant tension that exists between emotional man and homo mensor — man the measurer. These ambivalent tensions are reconciled within the environment of the game, in which the elements of emotion and rationality combine within a highly structured system of actions. It is not surprising, then, that a similar confluence exists in the folk speech of the participants. The emotions arising from the tension between player as personality and player as role representative, as well as from the inherent tensions existing in the antagonistic domain of competition, are channeled through the formal structure of the players' folk expressions, and mirror not only the values, norms, and anxieties of the baseball community, but those of the American culture in which the game is embedded. Maybe, after all is said and done, however, our real fascination in the game of baseball lies in the fact that, as San Francisco Chronicle columnist Herb Caen suggests (Caen 1983), "whereas we can not imagine ourselves executing a two-handed slam-dunk or a 50-yard field goal, we are still certain we have one base hit left in us."

NOTES

Chapter 1

1. See, for instance, *Work Hard and You Shall Be Rewarded. Urban Folklore from the Paperwork Empire.* Alan Dundes and Carl R. Pragter. Bloomington: Indiana University Press, 1975.

2. Psychologist John Edwards, in his article "The Home Field Advantage," comments that "Although such personalizations of the home field can only be carried so far, and although they may be regarded as unsportsmanlike, rumor in sports circles suggest that they are fairly common." (Edwards 1979:422)

3. See Ojo Arewa, E. and Alan Dundes, "Proverbs and the Ethnography of Speaking Folklore," *American Anthropologist* 66,6 part 2 (1964),70-85. This notion is also expressed in an article that presents an intriguing psychoanalytical approach to elephant jokes: Alan Dundes and Roger Abrahams. "On Elephantasy and Elephanticide." *The Psychological Review* 56(1969),225-241.

4. A perfect game is a game in which a pitcher retires every batter that he faces; no walks, no hits, no errors. That is, "Twenty seven men up, twenty seven men down".

Chapter 2

1. The definition of this last level is "Elimination games in which one participant after another is out and must wait until the game

is over before they can play again." I feel that it is a bit restrictive to limit the definition of "out-of-game" to apply only to players that must wait until the game is over before they can play, since, for instance, baseball players who are not in the game may be substituted into it.

2. It has been suggested by psychologist Jeffrey Goldstein that the reverse of this is also true. In his article "Outcome in Professional Team Sports: Chance, Skill, and Situational Factors" (Goldstein 1979:401-408) he states that "If the emphasis on winning is diminished, there should be a corresponding increase in the intrinsic motivations and satisfactions inherent in sports."

3. For an interesting discussion of the influence of the enviroment in sports, see John Edwards, "The Home Field Advantage," (Goldstein 1979:422).

Chapter 3

1. The theory of esoteric and exoteric groups was outlined by William Hugh Jansen in his essay "The Esoteric-Exoteric Factor in Folklore" which first appeared in *Fabula: Journal of Folktale Studies,* Vol. 2 (1959), 205-11. This essay is reprinted in Alan Dundes' *The Study of Folklore* (Dundes 1965).

2. These concepts are discussed at length in Richard Bauman's essay "Differential Identity and the Social Base of Folklore," in the *Journal of American Folklore,* Vol. 84, pp. 31-41.

Chapter 4

1. Coffin's reasoning behind this statement is that "ball players come from many different backgrounds, speaking many different ways." This is an unfortunate assertion in many ways, not the least of which is the assumption that the environment of the baseball team in no way affects a player's speech, that only his "background" — presumably meaning his original social and economic status - will influence his linguistic development. This is an absurd notion even in the most elementary treatment of folk

speech. The players are grouped for the purpose of a particular function (baseball) which is their defining element as a folk group and thus the focus of their folk speech. The status of the individual players in society is not an overriding concern to their position in the baseball community and thus is not of much importance. What is meant by "speaking many different ways" is very unclear. It is a moot point, however, as the primary concern is the persisting folk speech that exists within the baseball community and is learned by the players as they become a part of that community.

2. See also, John Edwards, "The Home Field Advantage," in *Sports, Games, and Play: Social and Psychological Viewpoints*, Jeffrey Goldstein, ed. New Jersey: Lawrence Erlbaum, 1979. pp. 409-438.

3. See, for instance William Labov, "The Art of Sounding and Signifying." in *Language and Its Social Setting*, ed. William Gage. pp. 84-116. Washington D.C.: Anthropolocigal Society of Washington; and Abrahams, Roger D. "Black Talking on the Streets," in *Explorations in the Ethnography of Speaking*, ed. Richard Bauman and Joel Sherzer. pp. 240-263. London: Cambridge University Press.

4. William Labov elaborates on the structural aspects of "signifying" and "sounding" in his essay "The Art of Sounding and Signifying," which appears in *Language and Its Social Setting*, ed. William Gage, 1974. pp. 84-116. Washington D.C.: Anthropological Society of Washington.

Chapter 5

1. Incidentally, this film is a funny and interesting look at a very formal English professor's first realization of, and attempt to collect, the slang of different folk groups.

Chapter 6

1. See, for instance, Lowell Cohen "A one word message," *The San Francisco Chronicle*, March 12, 1982. p.74.

Chapter 9

1.   This is also true in other folkgroups where quick, accurate communication is important. See, for instance, "The Folk Speech of United States Air Force Transport Pilots," Susan Gandell Kenagy, Master of Arts Thesis in Folklore, University of California at Berkeley. 1974. Another good example of this concision is evident in the communication between an infielder and an outfielder in a situation that demands that a ball hit to that outfielder be relayed to that fielder. Before the pitch, the fielder will turn around and remind the outfielder of this by saying, simply, "me and you".

Chapter 10

1.   Baseball taunting is often metonymous, the most common transformation being the substitution of "him" (the player) for the ball. Such metonymous usage can result in a variety of ways to say one thing. For instance, it is said of a good hitter that "He can stick", "He sticks", "He's got a stick" — all of which mean the same thing. Metonymous taunts single out the player as the object of attack, making the taunt a more direct reproach, as in "Put him in the book!", a statement of encouragement said to a pitcher (by his teammates) requesting him to get a player out, (with the result being logged in the scorebook). Other good examples are a "leg hit" in which a hitter runs out a slowly hit ground ball for a base hit, and "dip", which means chewing tobacco, so called because the act of getting it out of its container is called "dipping". There are many other interesting grammatical techniques used. The shortening of words is very common, as in "uni" for uniform, "vet" and "rook" for veteran and rookie, "slam" for grandslam, "ump" for umpire, and "chew" for chewing tobacco. Often a single letter, often that used in the scorebook, will be used to signify an event. A win becomes a "W", a strikeout is a "K", and a standing ovation is a "standing 'O'". There are also examples of onomatopoeic slang in which the term derives from the sound of the action, such as in "crack the ball" (hit it hard) and to "get plunked" (get hit with a pitch). This technique is most evident in the comment said when a player gets hit in the "cup", the protective metal device for the groin;

"ding-dong!". Acronymal forms are few, but include "ribby" for R.B.I. (run batted in).

2. This usage is discussed briefly by Alan Dundes in *Interpreting Folklore*. Bloomington: University of Indiana Press. p. 58.

3. See, for instance, *Deep Down in the Jungle: Negro Narrative from the Streets of Philadelphia*. Roger Abrahams, 1970. Chicago: Aldine.

BIBLIOGRAPHY

Abrahams, Roger D.
1968 Introductory Remarks to a Rhetorical Theory of Folklore. *Journal of American Folklore* 81:143-158.

Abrahams, Roger D.
1970 *Deep Down in the Jungle: Negro Narrative Folklore from the Streets of Philadelphia.* Chicago: Aldine.

Abrahams, Roger D.
1974 Black Talking on the Streets, in *Explorations in the Ethnography of Speaking,* ed. Richard Bauman and Joel Sherzer. pp. 240-263. London: Cambridge University Press.

Avedon, Elliott M. and Brian Sutton-Smith
1971 *The Study of Games.* New York: Wiley.

Bauman, Richard
1971 Differential Identity and the Social Base of Folklore. *Journal of American Folklore* 84:31-41.

Ben-Amos, Dan
1971 Towards a Definition of Folklore in Context. *Journal of American Folklore* 84:12.

Blumer, Herbert

1969 *Symbolic Interactionism.* New Jersey: Prentice-Hall.

Buckley, Walter

1967 *Sociology and Modern Systems Theory.* New York: Prentice-Hall.

Bouton, James

1970 *Ball Four.* New York: Dell.

Brunvand, Jan Harold

1978 *The Study of American Folklore* (2nd ed.). New York: Norton.

Burke, Kenneth

1961 *The Philosophy of Literary Form.* New York: Vintage Reprint Edition.

Burling, Robbins

1970 *Man's Many Voices.* New York: Holt, Rinehart, and Winston.

Caen, Herb

1983 Big Wide Wonderful World. *San Francisco Chronicle,* April 3, 1983. Sunday Punch, p.1.

Coffin, Tristram P.

1971 *The Old Ball Game.* New York: Herder and Herder.

Coser, Lewis

1956 *The Functions of Social Conflict.* Illinois: Free Press.

Deutsch, Helen

1926 A Contribution to the Psychology of Sport. *International Journal of Psycho-Analysis* 7:225.

Dorson, Richard M.

1971 *American Folklore and the Historian.* Chicago: University of Chicago Press.

Dundes, Alan

1965 *The Study of Folklore.* New Jersey: Prentice-Hall.

Dundes, Alan and Roger Abrahams

1969 On Elephantasy and Elephanticide. *The Psychoanalytic Review* 56 pp. 225-241.

Dundes, Alan

1975 *Analytic Essays in Folklore*. The Hague: Mouton.

Dundes, Alan

1978 *Essays in Folkloristics*. Meerut: Ved Vatuk.

Dundes, Alan

1980 *Interpreting Folklore*. Bloomington: University of Indiana Press.

Edwards, John

1979 The Home Field Advantage. in *Sports, Games, and Play: Social and Psychological Viewpoints*. ed. Jeffrey H. Goldstein. New Jersey: Lawrence Erlbaum. pp. 409-438.

Erikson, Erik H.

1977 *Toys and Reasons*. New York: Norton.

Flynn, Charles P.

1977 *Insult and Society*. New York: Kennikat.

Frank, Stanley

1941 Rough Riders of the Dugout. *Saturday Evening Post* 213 (May 17, 1941) pp. 18-19.

Freud, Sigmund

1960 *Group Psychology and the Analysis of the Ego*. New York: Bantam.

Freud, Sigmund

1960 *Jokes and Their Relation to the Unconscious*. trans. James Strachey, New York.

Freud, Sigmund

1963 *Character and Culture*. ed. Philip Rieff. New York: Collier.

Goldstein, Jeffrey H.

1979 *Sports, Games, and Play: Social and Psychological Viewpoints.* New Jersey: Lawrence Erlbaum.

Graham, Frank and Dick Hyman

1962 *Baseball Wit and Wisdom.* New York: Van Rees.

Guttman, Allen

1978 *From Ritual to Record.* New York: Columbia University Press.

Hawkes, Howard

1941 *Ball of Fire.* Produced by Samuel Goldwyn Co. Black and White, 35mm, 111 min.

Hemingway, Ernest

1952 *The Old Man and the Sea.* New York: Scribner's.

Hughes, Everett C.

1958 *Men and Their Work.* Illinois: Free Press.

Huizinga, Johan

1949 *Homo Ludens: A Study of the Play-Element in Culture.* London: Routledge and Kegan Paul.

Jansen, William Hugh

1959 The Esoteric-Exoteric Factor in Folklore. in *The Study of Folklore,* ed. Alan Dundes. pp. 43-51. New Jersey: Prentice Hall.

Klein, Melanie

1926 Infant Analysis. *International Journal of Psycho-Analysis* 7:61.

Labov, William

1974 The Art of Sounding and Signifying, in *Language in Its Social Setting,* ed. William Gage. pp. 84-116. Washington D.C.: Anthropological Society of Washington.

Laird, D.A.

1923 "Changes in motor control and individual variations under the influence of razzing," *Journal of Experimental Psychology* 6 (236-246).

Leach, Edmund

1964 Anthropological Aspects of Language: Animal Categories and Verbal Abuse, in New Directions in *The Study of Language,* ed. Eric Lenneberg. pp. 23-63. Cambridge: M.I.T. Press.

Le Bon, G.

1895 *Psychologie des Foules.* Paris.

Lee, Gretchen

1926 In Sporting Parlance. *American Speech* 1 (April 1926) pp. 369-370.

Levi-Strauss, Claude

1966 *The Savage Mind.* Chicago: University of Chicago Press.

Literary Digest, The

1913 Peril of the Baseball Lingo, *The Literary Digest* 47(Sept. 6, 1913). pp. 379-380.

Lorenz, Konrad

1966 *On Aggression.* New York: Harcourt, Brace, and World.

Maurer, David

1945 War and the Language, *The New Republic* 113 (Dec. 31, 1945) p. 908.

McDougall, W.

1920 *The Group Mind.* Cambridge.

Nation, The

1913 English and Baseball. *The Nation* 97 (Aug. 21, 1913) p. 161.

Novak, Michael

1976 *The Joy of Sports.* New York: Basic Books.

Partridge, Eric

1972 *Slang To-Day and Yesterday.* 4th ed. London: Routledge and Kegan Paul.

Redl, Fritz, Paul Gump, and Brian Sutton-Smith

1971 "The Dimensions of Games," in *The Study of Games* by Elliott M. Avedon and Brian Sutton-Smith. pp. 408-418. New York: Wiley.

Reston, James

1966 "Bouquet is Tossed at Sports," *Minneapolis Tribune,* October 8.

Ritter, Lawrence S.

1966 *The Glory of Their Times: The Story of the Early Days of Baseball Told by the Men Who Played It.* New York: Macmillan.

Samuels, V.

1927 Baseball Slang, *American Speech* (Feb., 1927) p. 256.

Smith, Leverett T.

1975 *The American Dream and The National Game.* Ohio: Popular Press.

Stokes, Adrian

1956 Psycho-Analytic Reflections on the Development of Ball Games. *International Journal of Psycho-Analysis* 37:185-192.

Toelken, Barre

1979 *The Dynamics of Folklore.* Boston: Houghton Mifflin.

Twain, Mark

1948 *A Connecticut Yankee in King Arthur's Court.* New York: Pocket Books.

Wallop, Douglass

1969 *Baseball: An Informal History.* New York: Norton.

Wentworth, Harold and Stuart Berg Flexner

1967 *Dictionary of American Slang.* New York: Thomas Crowell.

"When I come back you can tell me about the baseball."

Ernest Hemingway
The Old Man and the Sea.